S0-DZC-304

FROM DUST TO TRIUMPH:

REFLECTIONS FOR
A HOLY LENT

Lectionary Year B | Daily Office Year One

...in thanksgiving for nearly 175 years of raising up
a faithful priesthood for the Church.

PREFACE

The chief end of the church calendar is to remember, retrace, and even re-live the life of Jesus, so that we can live the life of Jesus. Whatever else it means "to keep a holy Lent," it is specifically to re-live one episode: Jesus' forty-day testing in the wilderness, in order to prepare us, as it prepared him, for the fateful events of Holy Week.

In one sense, we don't know much at all about those forty days. The gospel accounts of Christ's testing are spare, especially St. Mark's account, which we read on the first Sunday of Lent (1:9-15). But, as he so frequently does, Mark is suggesting more than he is telling us. He thinks that we should fill in the blanks, and so he tells of the episode as almost with a wink.

It is unlikely that the waters, wilderness, and "forty" are an accidental juxtaposition. And it is not an accident that everyone, it seemed—whether Essenes or Zealots, revivalists or survivalists—everyone who wanted a do-over for the people of God started it in the wilderness. So also with Jesus of Nazareth. The story of Jesus' wilderness sojourn begins like Israel's wilderness sojourn, with a passing through water—their exodus, his baptism. Their forty years of wilderness testing are reprised in his forty days of wilderness testing. In the waters that saved one "son" of God—"Out of Egypt I called my son" (Hosea 11:1; Matthew 2:15)—another Son of God is called to his Father's work. The wilderness that tested and formed a people to inhabit the land tested and formed a Person who would return to that land and call his people back to their God. Jesus is reliving the life of Israel, a new Israel in whom Israel is reborn and her hopes fulfilled.

If this is so, and if in Lent we re-live forty days in the wilderness to live the life of Jesus, then Lent might be about something more—even something else—than is often supposed. Our Lent is nothing less than our own preparation to be the children of Abraham, fulfilling the vocation given his people from the very beginning—to be a blessing to the nations, to put on display the goodness of God, to be a light to the nations reflecting the Light of the World.

We are wont to speak blithely of "giving something up for Lent." But Jesus gave something up to take something on. And, should we keep a holy Lent, so shall we.

GARWOOD P. ANDERSON, PhD
Dr. Anderson is the Professor of New Testament and Greek at Nashotah House Theological Seminary.

LENTEN
MEDITATIONS

MEDITATION ONE

FIRST PSALM: PSALM 95; PSALM 32; PSALM 143
SECOND PSALM: PSALM 102; PSALM 130
OLD TESTAMENT: JONAH 3-4
NEW TESTAMENT: HEBREWS 12:1-14
GOSPEL: LUKE 18:9-14

"Arise, go to Nineveh." Having disobeyed God when first called and left with the consequences of choosing his way over God's, Jonah returns begrudgingly to the path of life. Jonah will live, and after forty days of repentance, Nineveh will live too. Today the Church begins her annual journey of Lent, reminding us every step of the way that the grave could not hold Jesus and therefore cannot hold us, just as the belly of the fish could not hold Jonah. Like Jonah and Nineveh, it is never too late for us to return to the Lord who saves. The process may be painful, but the outcome glorious. We must die in order to live.

The Pharisee in Jesus's parable thanks God that he is "not like other men…even like this tax collector." And yet the tax collector goes "down to his house justified rather than the other." Jonah resented God's mercy for Nineveh and learned he needed it for himself. As we heighten our devotion over these weeks of Lent we may occasionally feel the same resentment: God loves the godless just as much as he loves us. And let us thank God that He does! We say our prayers, frequent the sacraments, read the Bible, and tend to the poor and needy; but these forty days of deeper devotion show us how far short we fall of God's righteousness. Our piety may be exemplary, pathetic, or somewhere in between; but none of us can stand before our judge in any other posture than that of the tax collector: "God, be merciful to me a sinner!"

Our common call both to holiness and humility is, however, far from doom and gloom. We glory in the cross of Christ, and we find great joy in this season. It is a thrill to realize that we need not have to act a certain way or say certain things of our own strength. We cannot save ourselves, and that is good news. "Lift your drooping hands and strengthen your weak knees," the author of Hebrews exhorts us. Thus we begin Ash Wednesday with upbeat Psalms: "Be glad you righteous, and rejoice in the Lord; shout for joy, all who are true of heart" (Ps. 32:12).

We end the day with patient certainty: "O Israel, wait for the Lord, for with the Lord there is mercy" (Ps. 130:6). We set off on the road to Calvary, willingly receiving discipline that seems "painful rather than pleasant," but remembering the promise of "the peaceful fruit of righteousness" won for the world by the risen Christ—a calling that drowns out Jonah's defiance, the Pharisee's self-righteousness, and our own manifold weakness. We remember today that we are dust—dust destined to live forever.

THE REV. ANDREW PETIPRIN

The Rev. Andrew Petiprin is Rector of St. Mary of the Angels Episcopal Church in Orlando, Florida. He was a Marshall Scholar at Magdalen College, Oxford and trained for ordination at Yale Divinity School. He is a member of the Cranmer Forum and a regular contributor to the Living Church magazine and the Covenant blog. He and his wife, Amber, have two young children, Alexander and Aimee.

MEDITATION TWO

FIRST PSALM: PSALM 37:1-18
SECOND PSALM: PSALM 37:19-40
OLD TESTAMENT: DEUTERONOMY 7:6-11
NEW TESTAMENT: TITUS 1
GOSPEL: JOHN 1:29-34

Often we are called to bring our hearts, minds, and bodies into the conformity that is taught by Christ. What would it mean in our day to be ready to confront false teachers? What would Paul have said if Titus were left behind to finish some work in our town? Would we be among those that are ready for leadership?

As we consider Titus, chapter 1, and who we are called to be as part of the Christian life, Paul provides a portrait of the character of those who are to oversee the church. This is not the first time Paul has articulated such significant criteria. We know that his is a consistent call crowned in the ability to teach sound doctrine.

Titus remains obedient to a call he had begun with Paul, having already spent much effort to have people ready for the call they are about to engage. These were people who had a willingness to serve Christ and were obedient to instruction and the authority given to Titus.

As we read in Deuteronomy, it is not a new thing that God's people are reminded to seek obedience. This reminder to Titus should bring us great hope that God fulfills his covenant. It is through his work that we are able to be obedient. Paul emphasizes to Titus that difficult times lay ahead, and there is a call to holy men and women of God to prepare for ministry.

In Deuteronomy the people are entering into the new land promised to their forefathers and in Titus it is a people to whom Jesus commanded that they go and preach and make disciples. The names and places are different, but the faithfulness of God to provide for those who hear his word and obey remains the same.

The admonition about what is called for in a leader is not simply go and find these "types of people," it implies that the criteria is already known. Paul's letter to Titus is not a simple plea to find people that are like that; instead a description of who we are to be. Whether we are called to the role of Titus or those who are to be appointed, let us seek to be obedient to the call of God and follow Paul's clear description to seek the Kingdom of God with our whole heart. May we do so knowing that it is God who sustains us.

JASON TERHUNE, '15

Jason Terhune is a senior Master of Divinity student at Nashotah House Theological Seminary. A Postulant for Holy Orders from the Episcopal Diocese of Tennessee, he is married to Rebecca and they have three sons. In June 2015, Mr. Terhune will assume the responsibilities of director of recruitment for Nashotah House. As they continue to enjoy life at the House, they look forward to God's calling for their future ministry.

MEDITATION THREE

FIRST PSALM: PSALM 95; PSALM 31
SECOND PSALM: PSALM 35
OLD TESTAMENT: DEUTERONOMY 7:12-16
NEW TESTAMENT: TITUS 2
GOSPEL: JOHN 1:35-42

"Look, here is the Lamb of God!" Here is the one for whom they will spread a net without a cause, the one against whom malicious witnesses will rise up, the one with whom they will exchange evil for good, the one against whom they will gather together, the one whom they will mock, the one whom they will tear to pieces and not stop until He is lifted up on a tree, crucified, dead, and buried.

"Look, here is the Lamb of God!" Here is the one who will hear the whispering of the crowd, who will know the fear of those who surround Him, will know the plot to take His life, but will give that life willingly, obediently, lovingly. Here is the one who will trust in the Lord completely, the one who will commit His spirit into His Father's hand—not to be redeemed by Him, but rather to redeem us.

"Look, here is the Lamb of God!" Here is the one who will maintain for us the covenant loyalty sworn by Abraham's descendants so long ago. Here is the one who will restore that broken covenant, who will let God's love and blessing rain down upon us, who will make us the most blessed of peoples through His sacrifice for us.

"Look, here is the Lamb of God!" Here is the one that we must come and see—the one Messiah. Here is the one who we must follow, from Bethlehem to Nazareth, to Jerusalem, to Golgotha, in the shadow of the cross, the shadow thrown by the light of the empty tomb.

"Look, here is the Lamb of God!" Here is the one who gave himself for us that He might redeem us from all iniquity and purify for himself a people of his own—a people that have walked the way of the cross with Him, a people who know that his tomb is empty, a people who know He is coming back.

"Look, here is the Lamb of God!" Here is the grace of God which has appeared, bringing salvation to all, training us to renounce impiety and worldly passions, and in the present age to live lives that are self-controlled, upright, and godly, while we wait for the blessed hope and the manifestation of the glory of our great God and Savior, Jesus Christ. Here is the one for whom we wait.

"Look, here is the Lamb of God!" Here is our Redeemer, our King, our Savior, our Lord.

Be strong and let your heart take courage, all you who wait for the Lord, for here is the Lamb of God!

THE REV. JILL STELLMAN, '12

The Rev. Jill Stellman serves as the priest-in-charge at Christ Episcopal Church, Herkimer, New York. She is focused on reaching out to a hurting community and ministering to those in need, spiritually and physically, inside and outside the church building. She and her husband, Paul Androski, a retired Army First Sergeant, have been married 18 years.

MEDITATION FOUR

First Psalm: Psalm 30; Psalm 32
Second Psalm: Psalm 42; Psalm 43
Old Testament: Deuteronomy 7:17-26
New Testament: Titus 3
Gospel: John 1:43-51

"Penitence," wrote Martin Thornton, "becomes a search for the truth of one's vocation" (The Purple Headed Mountain, Ch. 5). Penitence can take on this character when we accept the possibility, which the biblical revelation insists is fact, that all of God's creation is an integrated, purposeful, living unfolding with a unique role for each and every thing, including us. Certainly true penitence begins as Our Lord told Philip: "Follow me" (John 1:43). This becomes adventurous when it grows into a disposition of life: Be Following Him. If we are, in the phrase of English fourteenth-century writer, Walter Hilton, to reform into the likeness of Jesus, that journey of holiness begins in finding harmony with our surroundings, as Jesus surely had with His, and goes awry without it.

Perhaps the only valid test here is moral theology: have I committed fewer sins? Sin is separation, and paying lip service to the first line of the Nicene Creed is the height of Pride, the basis of all separation. Not only when receiving Communion, reciting the Office, or studying Scripture, but always and everywhere, are we choosing to follow—opening to, and in this sense, "thanking" —God Almighty as He actualizes in our lives? And do we use His creation and His creatures to His greater glory? For the revelation disallows any version of "God is not here and doesn't much care."

"Repent and be baptized," is how Peter exhorted the first Christians (Acts 2.38). But as Paul reminded Titus, our baptism is more than a rite; it is a way of life, a sacramental status before God. Peter might have urged, "Choose God and then spend the rest of your life working out the implications of that choice." Be baptized—just as we say, "be mature" or "be yourself:" our Lord demands we own our status, incorporated into Him "in virtue of his own mercy" (Ti. 3:5). Baptism plunges us into Trinitarian reality through the glory of material water, fragrant oil, and audible words. Within such paradox lies enough food for Lenten mystagogy several times over.

To wit: "You will see heaven opened, and the angels of God ascending and descending upon the Son of Man" (Jn. 1:51). It was St. Augustine who wrote, "Every visible thing in this world is put under the charge of an angel" (De diversis quaestionibus, 79). This staggering statement is also exemplary ascetical theology, the articulation of spiritual growth: for only through our sense perception is God's presence available to us. As God called Mary by sensible means of Gabriel, we are called by God aided by the angelic host who through the visible and perceivable bring the invisible and incomprehensible beckoning before us, inviting adventure anchored in Christ.

Mr. Matthew Dallman

Matthew Dallman is completing a Master of Theological Studies (MTS) in the Distance Learning program at Nashotah House, with a concentration in Anglican Studies. He has received an M.A. in Liturgy from Catholic Theological Union in Chicago. He is the founder and executive director of Akenside Press, a small publishing company that is reissuing all thirteen books by Anglican theologian Martin Thornton. Along with his wife, Hannah, and daughters Twyla, Oona, Isadora, and Marla, he prays at Saint Paul's Parish, Riverside, near Chicago, where he is also an adult catechist.

MEDITATION FIVE

FIRST PSALM: PSALM 63:1-8; PSALM 63:9-11; PSALM 98
SECOND PSALM: PSALM 103
OLD TESTAMENT: DEUTERONOMY 8:1-10
NEW TESTAMENT: 1 CORINTHIANS 1:17-31
GOSPEL: MARK 2:18-22

As we hit certain age milestones in our life, we have a tendency to become reflective. I am in my late 40s and have another milestone looming. I am told it really hits home when you open the mailbox and see the AARP card waiting for you. Introspection can be beneficial just as long as we do not become melancholy and allow our self-examination to turn into self-recrimination and pity or to feel that we have somehow reached the pinnacle. In our time here on earth, Lenten seasons come and go like so many other liturgical seasons rolling into the mists of time behind us. As we enter another Lent, it is important to our spiritual and psychological well-being to make it a productive time for reflection and for our relationship with God. At first this can seem to be self-centered, but it is through taking the time to address our spiritual health and relationship with our Creator that we become better spouses, parents, employees/employers, and messengers of the Gospel.

In our reading from Psalm 103, I am reminded today of some of the facets of our relationship with God that are worthy of reflection during Lent. The Psalmist begins with "Bless the Lord, O my soul, and all that is within me, bless His holy name!" Gratitude and blessing should arise from the depths of our soul and our very being for all that God is and all that He has done for us. The Psalmist goes on to enumerate some of those blessings to us: forgiveness, healing, redemption, satisfaction, loving kindness and mercy. We are reminded in verse 14 and 15 that we are dust and our days are like grass but we not only have hope, we have joy because "…the mercy of the Lord is from everlasting to everlasting on those who fear Him." No matter how long or how short our days on earth we are truly living our life as believers in a crescendo. It does not end here but goes on into eternity and glory with our Lord and Savior.

In 1 Corinthians 1:17, St. Paul discusses his focus and the fact that Christ sent him to "… preach the gospel, not with wisdom of words, lest the cross of Christ be of no effect." He goes on in 1 Corinthians 2:4 and 13 to discuss the power of the Holy Spirit in his preaching and life. During Lent, may we find renewed focus in our personal and spiritual lives and seek the wisdom and power of the Holy Spirit to live effectively for Christ.

THE VENERABLE DR. MYLES A. CALVIN

Dr. Calvin is the Executive Archdeacon for the Missionary Diocese of CANA West (Church of Nigeria/ACNA) and he also serves as a priest at the Anglican Cathedral Church of St. Francis in El Paso, Texas. In the past he has served as a military chaplain and is currently a chaplain in the US Air Force Auxiliary-Civil Air Patrol. He became a proud Associate Alumnus of Nashotah House in May 2011. Archdeacon Calvin's family includes Nancy who is an educator and they have two daughters, Monica and Christinia, and a son Jeremy.

MEDITATION SIX

FIRST PSALM: PSALM 41; PSALM 52
SECOND PSALM: PSALM 44
OLD TESTAMENT: DEUTERONOMY 8:11-20
NEW TESTAMENT: HEBREWS 2:11-18
GOSPEL: JOHN 2:1-12

What do you have that God has not given you? In both the Old Testament and Psalm readings for today, we are reminded of God's provision for all whom he created. We also read of the grave danger for those who fail to recognize the source of their blessings, believing that their strength, ability, and even their life is something other than the gracious gift of the Almighty.

Though I would not venture to call myself one who "forgets God", or a tyrant who "boasts of wickedness", how often do I find myself living as though God's provision is the result of my labor? How much quicker am I to bring petitions before the throne of grace than to return in praise and thanksgiving that God would even hear the concerns of his lowly creature whose very being depends solely on his continued love and mercy?

And yet, though we are powerless to help ourselves apart from God's grace, Jesus Christ shared in our humanity that we might partake of his resurrected humanity; and therefore "he is not ashamed to call us brethren".

Whether we are blessed with an epiphany of Christ like the wedding guests at Cana, or whether Christ's daily revealing of himself is found in his Sacraments and the reading of his Word, we must take heed that we remember by whose will we were created and have our being.

FROM DUST TO TRIUMPH: REFLECTIONS FOR A HOLY LENT

What do you have that God has not given you? Our wealth, our safety, our talents, our learning, our families, and our very lives would be naught apart from God. Yet, feeble as we are, God not only welcomes our petitions but lowered himself to live daily among us. He welcomes creatures of dust to become his sons and daughters and to partake in his eternity, having been made like unto God in the resurrection and ascension of Jesus Christ and our baptism into his Body.

What do you have that God has not given you? Nothing. To turn the question around, what has God withheld from us? Neither life, nor salvation, nor even his own Son has been denied us. Therefore, let us remember his commandments and his statues. As Mary said to the servants at Cana, "do whatever he tells you", and 'trust in the mercy of God for ever and ever, and give him thanks for what he was done'.

THE REV. ALEXANDER R. PRYOR, '14

The Rev. Alexander Pryor is Teaching Fellow in Church Music and Associate Director of Chapel Music at Nashotah House. Originally from Newfoundland, Canada, he lives on campus with his wife Kristina, and their young children Theophilus and Lorelai.

MEDITATION SEVEN

FIRST PSALM: PSALM 45
SECOND PSALM: PSALM 47; PSALM 48
OLD TESTAMENT: DEUTERONOMY 9:4-12
NEW TESTAMENT: HEBREWS 3:1-11
GOSPEL: JOHN 2:13-22

Lent is a time of preparation—an examination of conscience to ready ourselves for Christ. Today's readings remind me of the importance of staying focused on Jesus in all that I do. There is a song, Turn Your Eyes Upon Jesus, that plays in my head as I read the words of today's scriptures:

Turn your eyes upon Jesus
Look full, in his wonderful face
And the things of earth will grow strangely dim
In the light of his glory and grace

Keeping God in focus during our daily tasks is key to a deeper relationship with Him. Christ in our life is glorified by our enthusiasm and actions. As we look at ourselves, this is an area in particular to consider. Are our daily tasks, however tedious or mundane, done with Christ as center and with our eyes fully on Him?

Let's talk about joy, grace, and adoration. Have you ever met someone who doesn't smile much, complains a lot, and finds fault in most things? Whether that person lives on your street, or in your house or in the mirror, we have all encountered the cold rebellion of a hardened heart that is described in Hebrews 3:8. Be Christ for someone having a bad day. Exude His glory in all you say and do. Psalm 48 tells us, "Great is the Lord, and greatly to be praised." It is hard to have a harsh word when we focus our eyes on the greatness of the Lord. This does not mean when the puppy has an accident on the floor we cherish the moment with praises and thanksgiving. In a real world, things happen that discourage us, and a false joy during those times is neither helpful nor encouraging to others. It does mean that by looking to Jesus during trying situations we can address the fault, clean it up, and forgive the sin. My puppy craves my love and attention even with his faults. Christ craves our love and adoration in a way that lifts us up when we give it, even when the day has gone awry. Draw your mind to his presence and take refuge in Him and in His Word.

It is in your closeness to Jesus that you realize how trustworthy He is. To meet Christ face-to-face cannot be rushed. To be in His presence in between the one o'clock appointment and picking up the kids from school is not savoring the sanctity of intimacy. Intimacy is coming into His presence in peace and intentional contemplation. Being a faithful companion with Christ is a process that in our modern culture of haste is not always easy but can be achieved through prayer and living a life devoted to Christ.

MRS. MARCIA ALLISON

Marcia Allison, Spouse of the House, is married to the Rev. Roy Allison, '12. Fr. Allison is rector of St. Mark's Episcopal Church in Tampa, Florida. Marcia and Fr. Roy have two daughters, one of whom went through the process of seminary formation with them at Nashotah House and continues to live at home as she attends her first year of college. Marcia is a member of the Order of the Daughters of the King and the Order of St. Luke, respectively. She is also a trained iconographer.

LENTEN
MEDITATIONS

MEDITATION EIGHT

MORNING PSALM: 119:49-72
EVENING PSALMS 49, 53
OLD TESTAMENT: DEUTERONOMY 9:13-21
NEW TESTAMENT: HEBREWS 3:12-19
GOSPEL: JOHN 2:23-3:15

Our annual journey through Lent recapitulates the forty years' wanderings of the Hebrews on their way from Egypt to the Promised Land. The season's psalms and readings recall the Israelites' disobedience in the wilderness, as in the verses of Psalm 95 recited daily at Morning Prayer.

During their wanderings, the Israelites are repeatedly brought face to face with their propensity toward rebellion against God. Lent similarly asks us to confront the reality of our own sinfulness. During this season, we stand to learn much about ourselves from the biblical stories of "the day of temptation in the wilderness."

All three of today's Daily Office readings address this theme in different ways. The Letter to the Hebrews quotes Psalm 95 in solemn warning against "an evil, unbelieving heart, leading you to fall away from the living God." As a remedy against such sin, the readers should "exhort one another every day, as long as it is called 'today', that none of you may be hardened by the deceitfulness of sin."

In the reading from Deuteronomy, it is not mutual exhortation but the intercession of Moses that saves the people from God's wrath regarding their sin of idolatry in fashioning a golden calf to worship in God's place. Moses recounts, "Then I lay prostrate before the Lord as before, forty days and forty nights; I neither ate bread nor drank water, because of all the sin which you had committed, in doing what was evil in the sight of the Lord, to provoke him to anger."

The concluding verse of the Gospel reading from John draws on a later episode: "And as Moses lifted up the serpent in the wilderness, so must the Son of Man be lifted up, that whoever believes in him may have eternal life." This verse alludes to the story in Numbers 21, where the Lord sends lethal fiery serpents among the people as punishment for their grumbling and complaining. When the people repent and ask Moses to intercede for them, he fashions a bronze serpent, and mounts it on a pole, so that those bitten by the fiery serpents may look upon it and live. The mystery thus prefigured is that of Jesus lifted up upon the cross, so that sinners may look upon him in faith and be saved. Beyond mutual exhortation and intercession, here is God's ultimate remedy for sin.

JOHN D. ALEXANDER, MASTER'S IN SACRED THEOLOGY (STM), 2004
The Rev. John D. Alexander has been Rector of S. Stephen's Episcopal Church in Providence, Rhode Island, since 2000. He previously served parishes in Wayne, Pennsylvania, and Staten Island, New York. He received his M.Div. from Virginia Theological Seminary in 1992. In 2014, he received his Ph.D. in Christian Ethics from Boston University. Fr. Alexander serves as Superior of the North American Region of the Society of Mary. He and his wife Elizabeth are the proud parents of two grown sons.

MEDITATION NINE

FIRST PSALM: PSALM 50
SECOND PSALM: PSALM 59; PSALM 60; PSALM 19; PSALM 46
OLD TESTAMENT: DEUTERONOMY 9:23-10:5
NEW TESTAMENT: HEBREWS 4:1-10
GOSPEL: JOHN 3:16-21

"Offer to God a sacrifice of thanksgiving, and make good your vows to the Most High." Thus reads the first Offertory Sentence of the Book of Common Prayer, taken from today's Psalter reading. It is a phrase which we are likely accustomed to hearing in the liturgical context; yet this phrase is much more than a cue to send up the offering plates, it is in fact a prophetic and rousing call to again examine one's self before God.

Psalm 50 is divided into three main sections. The first, in verses 1-6, speaks of a divine courtroom, the temple, where God calls upon all those who have made a covenant with him in the presence of a sacrifice. Much like the passage in Genesis 4 between Cain and Abel, the primary question of the text is, "What is an acceptable sacrifice?"

Section two, in verses 7-14, and section three, in 15-23, deal with God's judgement against both Israel and the wicked. It is a mistake to separate these groups too definitively. Like Jesus' parable of the wheat and the tares, it seems that the two are a part of the same society and have even grown up in the midst of each other. The text itself proclaims them to be brothers.

God's reproof towards Israel is that they have trusted in their acts of sacrifice and not in the covenant that he maintains, resulting in confidence of self, pride, and not in thankfulness to God. Likewise

God's judgment against the wicked is that they live inconsistently with the scriptures they profess to believe. The final admonition of the text in verse 21 is both to "bring thanksgiving as a sacrifice" as well as to "go the right way." The same is echoed throughout the scriptures.

It is an odd notion, liturgically speaking, that we would place such a reexamination at this point in our Eucharistic narrative, since the gathered church would have ordinarily not only just made their Confession of Sin, but would also have given the Peace. Yet this phrase, the Offertory Sentence, is appropriately connected to the two former acts of contrition, repentance, and signaling of right-relationship among ourselves, God, and our neighbor. The gifts we bring to God are only rightly brought when our life is in agreement with his Word, spoken in the readings, and in thanksgiving that he has done for us what we could not do for ourselves.

Sometime today take a look at p. 376 of the Book of Common Prayer and meditate on the passages therein. No fewer than five of them contain some implicit call for self-examination, either in the verses themselves or in their immediate context. Ask yourself what sort of sacrifice are you bringing to God this season, and in what ways have you been long disobedient to his Word?

MR. LANCE M. LORMAND, '16

Mr. Lance M. Lormand is a postulant of the Episcopal Diocese of Fort Worth under the direction of the Rt. Rev. Jack Iker. He holds a Bachelor of Arts from Dallas Baptist University and a Master of Theological Studies from Truett Seminary. He is also a Chaplain Candidate in the United States Air Force with seven years of combined military service. Lance and his wife, Danielle, were married in September of 2012.

MEDITATION TEN

FIRST PSALM: PSALM 95; PSALM 40; PSALM 54
SECOND PSALM: PSALM 51
OLD TESTAMENT: DEUTERONOMY 10:12-22
NEW TESTAMENT: HEBREWS 4:11-16
GOSPEL: JOHN 3:22-36

Today's readings have a common theme: the supremacy of God. John 3: 22-36 strikes a strong chord in today's world. Here we see Jesus and John the Baptist, baptizing people into two different baptisms. John's is a baptism of repentance and cleansing, and Jesus' a baptism of new and unending life. The difference in the baptisms is not the focus. John's reaction to the statement, "Rabbi, he who was with you across the Jordan, to whom you bore witness—look, he is baptizing, and all are going to him.'" John's disciples are wondering what is John going to do about this?

Jesus is stealing John's thunder! John's response is eloquent and humble: "He must increase, but I must decrease." How often do we allow our own pride to get in the way of recognizing how our Lord Jesus Christ is acting through us? How often do we focus on how we must increase and forget that our purpose in this life is to further the kingdom of Christ, and not to glorify ourselves? We are called to bring people to Christ so that he can transform them, and use them for His glory. We love to be complimented; we love to be recognized when we achieve something. I dare say that those needs are not a bad thing, but the question we must ask in all we do is—am I doing this for me, for my benefit, for my glorification? Or am I doing this to the glory of God, for the glory of God, and with the understanding that my actions are not to increase myself, but to increase His kingdom?

When we engage our lives, our work, and our relationships, intertwining them with what glorifies God, we give up the need for recognition, and avoid the pitfalls of pride. The difficulty is maintaining that mindset, and recognizing that in all the good and bad that comes to us in this transitory life, because of God's grace, he is there and his will is glorious. This is how we decrease. We live for God through the power of his Holy Spirit, in faith, and always allowing our testimony to be communicated through our words and actions. God is calling us to decrease so that he might increase his kingdom in us and through us.

Mr. Christian Wood, '16

Mr. Christian Wood is married to Katherine, and they have two children Maggie-Jane, age 5 and Michael, age 2. Christian served for five years as Youth Minister at Church of the Redeemer in Sarasota, Florida, and is a seminarian from the diocese of Southwest Florida. A native of Queens, New York, Christian loves to engage people on a personal level and develop relationships. He says, "It is through relationships that Jesus taught his disciples, and is it through relationships I believe God uses me most effectively to spread His message of salvation and everlasting life."

MEDITATION ELEVEN

FIRST PSALM: PSALM 55
SECOND PSALM: PSALM 138; PSALM 139:1-17; PSALM 139:18-23
OLD TESTAMENT: DEUTERONOMY 11:18-28
NEW TESTAMENT: HEBREWS 5:1-10
GOSPEL: JOHN 4:1-26

Miles of steep climbs and pathless moorland lay between me and the nearest drink. I slogged on with my empty water bottles and tried to recall why I'd decided to walk twenty-five miles in the Brecon Beacons of South Wales on one of the hottest days of the year. Hadn't two Special Air Service (SAS) recruits just died from dehydration a couple of weeks before in almost the same spot? A lovely walk among the green slopes thus ended with my mind too preoccupied with my dry mouth to delight in my surroundings.

"I thirst." There's a reason, I believe, why John chose that brief confession as among the last words of Jesus to preserve. Earlier in his Gospel, Jesus had proclaimed to the Samaritan woman at the well that he is "living water" that would "well up to eternal life" for anyone who drank. For her, a woman thirsting for acceptance, perhaps also for forgiveness, those words opened her heart and mind to a new life. She drank from Christ something unlike anything she'd ever tasted before: something so powerful that it even made her forget the age-old animosity between Samaritans like her and Jews like this stranger she met at the well. In that brief encounter, she drank deeply—unwillingly and sceptically at first—but deeply all the same and in that drinking she found life.

But see how later, hanging on the cross, the Well of Eternal Life himself came to thirst. While that fact should add to the bleak poignancy of the cross, it shouldn't be all that surprising. The Samaritan woman had also found Jesus thirsty; his opening words to her were "Give me a drink." Noting this, St. Augustine writes, "The Samaritan woman at the well perceived the Lord's thirst, and her own thirst was satisfied by the one who thirsted; she initially became aware of him as a thirsty man that he might drink her as she came to believe. And on the cross he cried 'I am thirsty', though they had no intention of giving him what he longed for. For he was thirsting for them..." (En. Ps. 61.9)

We see in these two episodes that our own thirst, the deep desires of our parched and restless souls, is met by a thirsty Savior; we thirst to be at rest in him while he thirsts to "drink" us into him and his own life. Thus, when we turn to him 'in spirit and in truth', we find that the "living waters of eternal life" spring from a profound communion of thirst. As St. Bonaventure recognized, the "fountain fullness" of God's own love springs, paradoxically, from his own poverty. Thus, unlike me during the final leg of my walk, we find in God's overflowing poverty, from the spring of his thirst, the eternally satisfying delight that quenches even the deepest thirst.

THE REV. MARK CLAVIER

A native of South Carolina, the Rev. Mark Clavier is Acting Principal at St Michael's College, Llandaff, the training arm of the Church in Wales. He is currently serving on the committee tasked with establishing a new provincial training institution for the Church in Wales, of which St Michael's College will be part. Mark has published two books: Rescuing the Church from Consumerism (SPCK) and Eloquent Wisdom: Rhetoric, Cosmology and Delight in the Theology of Augustine of Hippo (Brepols). Fr. Clavier, his wife Diane, and their son Paul have lived in the United Kingdom since 2008.

Meditation Twelve

First Psalm: Psalm 24; Psalm 29
Second Psalm: Psalm 8; Psalm 84
Old Testament: Jeremiah 1:1-10
New Testament: 1 Corinthians 3:11-23
Gospel: Mark 3:31-4:9

The readings assigned for this second Sunday in Lent invite us to engage the Lenten discipline of critical self-reflection. Referencing 1 Corinthians 3, the late Bishop of Liverpool, Francis Chavasse, reminds us that "Man is likened in Holy Scripture to a Temple created for the dwelling of the Holy Spirit, and we must go through the chambers of that temple to see if there be anything there to offend our divine Guest." Though a seemingly simple and basic exercise, the ability to know ourselves and grow in virtue is nothing short of a life-long pursuit.

St. Paul's words in his first letter to the Church in Corinth help guide us into a truly Christian understanding of self-knowledge. As he says in 3:18— "Let no one deceive himself. If anyone among you thinks that he is wise in this age, let him become a fool that he may become wise." In a few simple words St. Paul reminds us of the ease with which we deceive ourselves, especially as it relates to our ability to self-diagnose our condition. While we as Christians can affirm the aphorism "know thyself," we should at the same time be critical of the accuracy of our self-diagnosis. Instead, as St. Paul says in verse 20, a true assessment of our condition is always to be found in God's searching presence—"…the Lord knows the thoughts of the wise, that they are futile." We see this theme of divine knowledge repeated in our reading from Jeremiah 1:5—"Before I formed you in the womb I knew you."

The Collect for the second Sunday of Lent begins with the words, "Almighty God, who seest that we have no power of ourselves to help ourselves." In keeping with the Pauline tradition, the church has always called its members to be wary of self-reliance. However, Scripture exhorts us not to despair but to place our hope and trust fully in the goodness and mercy of God. It is for this reason that this same collect can confidently beseech the Lord to "keep us both outwardly in our bodies, and inwardly in our souls." This is a picture of true self-reflection, for it leads us personally and corporately as the church to build our foundation solely upon the death and resurrection of Jesus Christ.

As Christians, may we have the courage to know ourselves as we truly are, not as we wish or imagine ourselves to be. If we can do this, rather than despairing at the sight of our brokenness and need, we can instead approach Easter with renewed gratitude and wonder as we encounter afresh the love of God displayed in his Son, Jesus Christ our Lord. It is then that we will truly know what the Rev. William Law (1686-1761) once called the "two great pillars" of our faith, "namely, the greatness of our fall and the greatness of our redemption."

THE REV. GENE W. (TRIPP) PRINCE, III

The Rev. Gene W. (Tripp) Prince, III serves as the Director of Family Ministry at Christ Church, Plano. Prior to this, he was the Associate Rector at Grace Anglican Church in Fleming Island, Florida. Before going into ordained ministry, Fr. Prince worked in communications and project management for several non-profit organizations. He has also led or participated in ministry trips to the United Kingdom, South East Asia, the Middle East, and South America. Fr. Prince lives in Plano, Texas with his lovely wife, Rachel, and their three children, Lillian, Emmeline, and Charlie.

Meditation Thirteen

First Psalm: Psalm 56; Psalm 57; Psalm 58
Second Psalm: Psalm 64; Psalm 65
Old Testament: Jeremiah 1:11-19
New Testament: Romans 1:1-15
Gospel: John 4:27-42

When I was an undergraduate philosophy student, I had a professor who told us, "You can trust me, but only for so long." By this he meant that his role as a teacher was to bring us to a place where we no longer had to accept his word on everything, but could engage the ideas, questions, and problems we encountered for ourselves. In fact, the more classes I had with this professor, the less he presented himself as a learned authority on philosophy and the more honest he became about his own questions and struggles with the discipline he taught. The result was that we as students were forced to understand the material better and were allowed to come to our own insights and conclusions.

Today's reading from the Gospel according to John shows a similar shift in how the people of Sychar encountered Jesus. It began with the testimony of a notoriously sinful woman: "He told me all that I ever did" (Jn. 4:39). While many Samaritans from the city believed in Jesus on account of this witness, many more put their faith in him after spending two days in his presence. We can probably assume that those who had already accepted the woman's testimony also found their conviction strengthened during that time.

All of us have, on some level, experienced this in our own relationship with Christ. Many of us were brought up in the Christian faith held by our parents, but a point came when we had to take ownership of this for ourselves. Even those of us who became Christians in adulthood had to rely on someone else's witness to Christ before we were willing to put our trust in him. Among other things, Christian maturity involves deepening our personal commitment to Christ and relying less on "external forces" to define our identity in him.

The season of Lent offers us a yearly opportunity to grow in this way. The liturgical calendar marches on, and the church will, through its rites and ceremonies, walk with Jesus to Jerusalem, to the cross, and finally to the empty tomb. But each of us must decide if we will be mere spectators at these events, or if we will seek to share more deeply in the death and resurrection of Christ. This, after all, is what it means to believe in Jesus, and it is our Christian duty, not just Lent after Lent, but day after day, as we turn from sin and selfishness and seek the renewal of his grace in our lives. The more we experience this new life in Christ, the more truly we know "that this is indeed the Savior of the world."

THE REV. MATTHEW KEMP, '13

The Rev. Matthew Kemp, '13, serves as the Curate at Christ Cathedral in Salina, Kansas in the Diocese of Western Kansas. He devotes much of his energy to teaching and writing, both within and outside the parish setting. He and his wife Alethea have two daughters, Theodora and Macrina.

Meditation Fourteen

First Psalm: Psalm 61; Psalm 62
Second Psalm: Psalm 68:1-20; Psalm 68:21-23; Psalm 68:24-35
Old Testament: Jeremiah 2:1-13
New Testament: Romans 1:16-25
Gospel: John 4:43-54

During Lent we read Scripture passages that speak to our particular situation in life, and those passages tend to take a penitential tone. Our reading from Jeremiah 2 provides us with the opportunity to see our lives framed by Israel's experience with God.

In this passage we see the LORD assessing Israel's relationship to Him. Israel was chosen by God and was delivered from slavery in Egypt. God gave Israel the land He promised to Abraham, Isaac, and Jacob. But Israel lost the devotion of her youth and went astray. Knowing that "whatever was written in former days was written for our instruction, that by steadfastness and by the encouragement of the scriptures we might have hope" (Rom. 15:4), we are driven to reflect on our relationship with the Lord. And as the years unfold, we see how that relationship has endured the tumults and triumphs of life. We remember the first zeal with which we sought the Lord as we entered into the great unknown Christian life. But that zeal tends to fade. We remember sunny mountain tops and dark valleys, and in both instances, instead of looking to the Lord for strength and salvation, we have looked elsewhere. We have become distracted and gone after things that we knew were worthless and destructive. But we pursued them anyway. We got off track and left our first love. We abandoned God, even though He never abandoned us.

Where have we forsaken the Lord and gone our own way? Where have we left the fountain of living waters for a broken cistern of stagnant water? Do we even notice that we are no longer close to the One who saved us and set us free from sin and death? Can we sense the bitter taste of stale water and return to the fountain of living waters? "O taste and see that the Lord is good! Happy is the man who takes refuge in him!" (Ps. 34:8).

As almost two weeks have passed since Ash Wednesday and we are in the midst of preparing to remember the death and to celebrate the resurrection of our Lord, let us be reminded of the ways in which we have forsaken Him and gone after things that profit not. Let us exchange our broken cisterns for the fountain of living water. And let us also have hope in our Lord who is always faithful so that we might "with confidence draw near to the throne of grace, that we may receive mercy and find grace in time of need" (Heb. 4:16).

MR. JOHN EDWARD FIELDING TRENUM, '15

John (Jedd) Trenum is in his senior year at Nashotah House. He and his wife Emily enjoy hiking, traveling, making new friends, and red wine. After graduation they will move to northern Virginia to serve in the Anglican Diocese of the Mid-Atlantic.

LENTEN
MEDITATIONS

MEDITATION FIFTEEN

FIRST PSALM: PSALM 72
SECOND PSALM: PSALM 119:73-96
OLD TESTAMENT: JEREMIAH 3:6-18
NEW TESTAMENT: ROMANS 1:28-2:11
GOSPEL: JOHN 5:1-18

"…do you presume on the riches of his kindness and forbearance and patience, not knowing that God's kindness is meant to lead you to repentance? But because of your hard and impenitent heart you are storing up wrath for yourself on the day of wrath when God's righteous judgment will be revealed."   *~Romans 2:4-5*

Did you catch that? For the longest time, I didn't. In fact, I might go so far as to say that for the longest time I thought just the opposite! One more time: "…God's kindness is meant to lead you to repentance…" God's kindness. Leads to repentance.

I always thought that anger led to repentance. At least that's how it worked when I was growing up. I did something wrong, something injurious or disrespectful, and then when things blew up (or, rather, when someone blew up: my Mom or Dad or a friend) then, and only then, I repented. Anger led to repentance. Or, a bad outcome led to repentance: I messed up at a job, didn't get the results I wanted or needed, and I repented of my failure to the person who had entrusted the task to me.

But I'm not so sure those were instances of real repentance. At least not repentance that leads to amendment of life, a true change of heart.

In Luke chapter 15, the story of the prodigal son, we see this truth played out. The son has rejected his family, rebelled against expectation, and then squandered the riches he had. A bad outcome—winding up having to eat pig slop—led to what looked like repentance.

But not really. At first, the younger son was still conniving. "I'll go to my father, and say the right things, and he'll give me a job. No more pig slop!" That isn't real repentance. Not until his dad comes running out to meet him, falls all over him, rejoices at his return in spite of the fact that he had blown the family fortune, and accepts him, not as a slave or employee, but as a son. Kindness. Then, and only then, does the son truly repent. "I'm not worthy to be called your son." No plan, no agenda, no scheme. The father's kind kisses lead to the son's broken heart, and true repentance. That, it seems to me, is exactly what St Paul means when he writes, "…God's kindness is meant to lead you to repentance…"

When someone has wronged me, kindness is the last thing on my mind. Vengeance? Yes. Anger? Absolutely. And those may lead to a version of repentance that cleans up a mess. But repentance that leads to the transformation of a heart? The reordering of an entire life? Only kindness can lead to that.

THE REV. CHIP EDGAR

Fr. Chip Edgar has been the Rector of Church of the Apostles, Columbia, South Carolina, since March 2004. Fr. Edgar and his wife, Beth, have five children. "It can be kind of a zoo at our house," he says, "but my family is my greatest joy. I am so proud of my kids. And I resonate with St. John when he wrote, 'I have no greater joy than this: to hear that my children are walking in the truth' (3 John 4)."

MEDITATION SIXTEEN

FIRST PSALM: PSALM 70; PSALM 71
SECOND PSALM: PSALM 74
OLD TESTAMENT: JEREMIAH 4:9-10; JEREMIAH 4:19-28
NEW TESTAMENT: ROMANS 2:12-24
GOSPEL: JOHN 5:19-29

In John 5:16-30, Jesus is accused of violating the Jewish prohibition of working on the Sabbath day because of his earlier healing of the crippled man by the Bethesda pool. How will Jesus defend himself against this charge? By identifying his work with that of his Father's. The prohibition of work on the Sabbath is grounded in the memory of God resting on the seventh day from his work of creation and making the day holy, and Moses commanded the Israelites to be like God by resting on this day. But what exactly did God rest from? Surely, without his providence sustaining the cosmos on the Sabbath, all would cease to be. If a child is born on the Sabbath, is not God the one who has granted that new life to us? Despite God's resting, Jewish tradition understood that there were some things that He alone still maintained, in order for the world to keep ticking. Jesus is claiming that his work of healing is akin to the work that only the Father can do on the Sabbath. "If you have a problem with what I am doing," he is saying, "take it up with my Father. I'm only doing the work that I learned from Him. If you're surprised now, just wait until you see what other work my Father has given me to do. It is no wonder that Jesus' claim of having the right that only God has provokes the religious authorities to violence.

Meditation on this passage during the season of Lent helps us see the narrative in a broader context that extends to us today. Jesus is here portrayed as healer, and as judge. As we fast and prepare ourselves for Holy Week and Easter, let us recognize the roles that Jesus plays. For the Lenten worshipper, meditating on Jesus role as judge shakes us out of a complacent stupor, our often unconscious sentiment that we are living a "good enough" life that will (hopefully, probably, maybe?) fall in line with the kind of life that Jesus says will be vindicated in the "hour" that is coming. For the Lenten worshipper, meditation on Jesus as healer is to see the way that the Church calendar is set up to be a microcosm of our world's story. As Lent anticipates Easter, and the first fruits of the healing of our world in Jesus' resurrection, so life as we know it today, with all of its pain and evil and suffering, anticipates the healing of all that is.

MR. RYAN POLLOCK, '17

Mr. Pollock is a postulant in the Episcopal Diocese of Dallas, Texas, where he served as member of the Fellows Initiative at the Church of the Incarnation. He and his wife, Jess, are enjoying their new home in Wisconsin.

Meditation Seventeen

First Psalm: Psalm 95; Psalm 69:1-23;
Psalm 69:24-30; Psalm 69:31-36
Second Psalm: Psalm 73
Old Testament: Jeremiah 5:1-9
New Testament: Romans 2:25-3:18
Gospel: John 5:30-47

How is the Christian to think about justice, especially when we know the achievement of such an end runs through the heart of our own brokenness as well? Throughout the epistles of the New Testament, there is an interpretive difficulty in understanding justice and how it is fleshed out. Indeed, common hermeneutical debates, especially in Pauline studies, revolve around the difference between justice, on the one hand, and righteousness, on the other. The debate is not helped by the fact that the Hebrew concept of shalom often overlaps semantically in meaning with righteousness and justice as understood in the New Testament.

Yet, despite our confusion around justice and our own complicity in injustice, the would-be-follower of Christ is beckoned unto a vocation of justice. Wendell Berry understands this well when he writes, "The two ideas, justice and vocation, are inseparable.... It is by way of the principle and practice of vocation that sanctity and reverence enter into the human economy. It was thus possible for traditional cultures to conceive that 'to work is to pray'" (*The Idea of a Local Economy*, p. 258).

And it is precisely in this place of prayer when we are most clearly tuned into the vocation of justice. The Psalmist says nothing less:

> For all day long I have been plagued, and am punished every morning. But when I thought how to understand this, it seemed to me a wearisome task, until I went into the sanctuary of God; then I perceived their end (Ps. 73:16-17).

It is fundamentally in the place of prayer—not the board room, nor the war room—where we rightly perceive God's justice. When the Psalmist looked to the end of the wicked, he was comforted. He was comforted because he had confidence in the God who would "put the world to rights," as the British are wont to say.

But the Psalmist was also put in his place, which is to say, he was humbled to the point of having mercy towards his enemies because he knew their end and also saw his own end…without God's mercy.

In 1949, C.S. Lewis spoke to this inextricable link between justice and mercy when he wrote:

> Mercy, detached from Justice, grows unmerciful. That is the important paradox. As there are plants which will flourish only in mountain soil, so it appears that Mercy will flower only when it grows in the crannies of the rock of Justice: transplanted to the marshlands of mere Humanitarianism, it becomes a man-eating weed, all the more dangerous because it is still called by the same name as the mountain variety (*God In The Dock*, p. 294).

Therefore, like the Psalmist, let us be encouraged and press onward as people who trust deeply in God's justice but are moved to mercy in the present…yes, even towards our enemies.

THE REV. CLINT WILSON, '13

Fr. Clint Wilson is a Curate for Young Family, Youth and College ministry at the Church of St. David of Wales in Denton, TX (Episcopal Diocese of Dallas). His wife, Theresa, is a student affairs professional at the University of North Texas.

Meditation Eighteen

First Psalm: Psalm 75; Psalm 76
Second Psalm: Psalm 23; Psalm 27
Old Testament: Jeremiah 5:20-31
New Testament: Romans 3:19-31
Gospel: John 7:1-13

"They are justified freely by his grace as a gift" (Rom. 3:24). Doesn't it just make life so much easier knowing that we are justified freely by his grace through the redemption that came by Christ Jesus? Does being justified by grace mean that we have no part to play in salvation?

A priest recently told me, "Live without murmuring." Murmuring goes on quite a bit within our souls. My soul. "As a Christian, your life is full of grace. But receiving grace is sometimes messy."

Mess, I know mess. Really, I know mess. The Oxford English Dictionary defines mess as one of two meanings. The first, "an untidy state of things." Very helpful. The second, "A collection of things causing such a state." Equally as helpful. Neither definition should imply any dismay, though.

St. Benedict's rule of food (Rule of Benedict, Ch. 39) assumes a level of messy grace. Eating with your friends, your family, or your enemies, is rarely pretty. Children must be corrected, friends' elbows are ignored, and your enemies? Well, you're supposed to be praying for them, aren't you?

Benedict understood the idea of messy grace. It is charity. There will be two kinds of food, because of your picky brethren; there will be a selection of food reserved by the Cellarer; otherwise we know we would eat it all. He understood that young children must begin with a bit of food because those stomachs are smaller than the eyes. With the psalmist in today's reading, we remember we serve he who is radiant, majestic, making vows to him and fulfilling them. One step at a time. The "messiness" of grace — ours or our neighbors' — is about how God continues to work in our lives. Life does not become easier; instead, we become more observant and active in how we see grace working in our lives.

As we are less than a month away from the hope that is Easter, let us repent and return – fallen, faithful, forgiven, never losing Him. And yes indeed, justified. Yes — you — are justified freely in Christ Jesus, our Lord, our 'very full comfort'. Amen.

REBECCA TERHUNE, '15

Rebecca Terhune is finishing her MTS degree as we speak. She hails from the Diocese of Tennessee with her husband, Jason, who is a postulant for holy orders. They are the happy parents to three sons. When she is not working on The Missioner magazine or writing papers for Fr. Holtzen, she may be seen chasing her black Labrador, Bonnie Kate, out of the nearby Nashotah woods.

MEDITATION NINETEEN

FIRST PSALM: PSALM 93; PSALM 96
SECOND PSALM: PSALM 34
OLD TESTAMENT: JEREMIAH 6:9-15
NEW TESTAMENT: 1 CORINTHIANS 6:12-20
GOSPEL: MARK 5:1-20

One of God's greatest blessings to the human race is the miracle that the Holy Scriptures of the Old and New Testaments are relevant to every time and place. In the appointed readings, we observe that human nature has actually changed very little since the days of the Prophet Jeremiah or of the Savior. We are self-righteous. We suffer from moral blindness. We are critical of others but judge our own behavior to be righteous. Again and again we regard everything we do as forgivable, and we cut ourselves slack, but we have little mercy for others. This mercilessness goes hand-in-hand with our greed: We often ache for satisfactions that do not belong to us, or for pleasures we have not earned. In all of this we long for salvation and something to sing about.

Another spiritual difficulty is when we have made that most important decision to follow the Lord, but we are determined to follow Him on our own terms. The account of the Gergesene demoniac illustrates this phenomenon. The text does not say what drove the poor man to the tombs, but I suspect that it was the same alienating powers that drive you and me there: inordinate desires, lack of concern for others, too much concern for mostly imagined needs, or the sloth that avoids the repentance that opens the heart to love. Too often we want too much too soon, which is evidence that our God-given reason is being ignored. Notice that the fleeing demons found their kind in pigs.

But in spite of all this mess he's in; in spite of his hating the Help now come to lift him out of the graveyard, the Gergesene experiences an unexpected manifestation of divine power. The greed-demons flee, leaving the man himself. Changed for ever, the man wants to follow Jesus now. But the Lord replies, "Go home to your friends and tell them how much the Lord has done for you." The Changed Man returned to those who had known and pitied him. What did he say to them? I believe he said again and again, "Jesus saves." And I imagine from personal experience that his constant prayer was: "Thank you, Lord Jesus!" Such simple words did change the world once and still can. The Gergesene surely discovered what we too discover when we are obedient and eager to serve the Lord: that the Father and the Son come into us to celebrate a feast.

Is it not the case that American Christians are especially susceptible to the desire to enjoy the benefactions of the Lord's near presence before we have done our Christian duty? The more we realize that we really are part of the Body of Christ in this world, and that the Spirit of God does indeed dwell in our flesh and blood, the more we will gladly go back to our own people and speak of what the Lord has done.

THE REV. W.L. CHIP PREHN, PH.D. '85

HEADMASTER OF TRINITY SCHOOL, MIDLAND, TEXAS

Chip Prehn graduated from Nashotah House and was ordained to the diaconate and priesthood in 1985. Married to Celia Jones of Dallas, the Prehns have three almost grown children. Chip was a parish priest for twelve years in Dallas, Philadelphia, and San Antonio before entering school work in 1996. He earned the Ph.D. in the History of American Education in 2005 from the University of Virginia and is Headmaster of Trinity School, Midland, Texas.

MEDITATION TWENTY

FIRST PSALM: PSALM 80
SECOND PSALM: PSALM 77; PSALM 79
OLD TESTAMENT: JEREMIAH 7:1-15
NEW TESTAMENT: ROMANS 4:1-12
GOSPEL: JOHN 7:14-36

In 1630, the great Dutch artist Rembrandt painted a depiction of Jeremiah the prophet. The prophet sits with his head in his hand, surrounded by an almost tangible darkness. His eyes are downcast, and carved into his face are nearly five decades of tireless preaching and teaching and ministry. Jerusalem, barely visible in the background, drowns in flames. The prophet stares out into the darkness in utter desolation, earning his nickname "the weeping prophet."

The Israelites, it seems, had fallen into a kind of external faith in the covenant of God. They saw their Temple, that incredible structure, as incontrovertible proof of the blessing and affirmation of God. But Jeremiah was entrusted with some bad news: the external signs of God's covenant are not the heart of the matter. They are gifts from God for the building up of His chosen people. But God's real gift was never just the Temple—it was Himself. The Temple was important because of what it contained, not because it remained. It was not to remain standing for long. God's ultimate gift is always and only Himself.

As we walk through this season of fasting and prayer, we must ask ourselves: Are there external signs of our covenant with God, our relationship with God, that we have begun to trust as the Israelites trusted the Temple? Is it, perhaps, the fact of our ordination? Our disciplined lives of prayer? The many sacrifices we've made for the priesthood? Do we cry, like the Israelites, "This is the temple of the Lord, the temple of the Lord, the temple of the Lord…"?

Jeremiah would have us remember this well: the faith that we profess cannot be possessed. For who can possess God? He is beyond definition, beyond comprehension, beyond our wildest imagination. He cannot be possessed, but He can be pursued. And Jeremiah promises that the desolation of Jerusalem can be averted by our return to God.

We know that this weeping prophet prefigures another Prophet, who also carried a great burden of suffering. He walked the Via Dolorosa to a cross. The Lord spoke through Jeremiah, that the people must "Go now to…where I made my Name dwell at first." Go back to the beginning. Christ, of course, is our beginning; He is the One to whom we must return. This Lent can be the time of our return. In the words of St. Benedict of Nursia, "Always we begin again."

THE REV. JOE HERMERDING, '09

Fr. Joe serves as Associate Rector for Children and Family Ministry at Church of the Incarnation in Dallas, Texas. He and his wife Ellora have three children.

MEDITATION TWENTY-ONE

FIRST PSALM: PSALM 78:1-39
SECOND PSALM: PSALM 78:40-72
OLD TESTAMENT: JEREMIAH 7:21-34
NEW TESTAMENT: ROMANS 4:13-25
GOSPEL: JOHN 7:37-52

"But this command I gave them, 'Obey my voice, and I will be your God, and you shall be my people; and walk in all the way that I command you, that it may be well with you'" (Jer. 7:23).

Speak Lord, your servant listens. Every day of our life, we are bombarded with sound bites of one kind or another. Radio, television, Facebook, YouTube, phone alerts, texts, computers and various other forms of communication and entertainment flood our life. How can I discern God's voice and His call to me when the world and the noise in it seem to drown out all else? How many times have we heard other folks say that they have to leave their own house and plan a getaway so that they might escape all of the noise of life and listen for God's voice? We are a people who are surrounded by the noise of the world and at times one can only be heard by shouting louder than one's neighbor. Few restaurants today are quiet places to enjoy a meal together. I walk into most restaurants and there is concert volume sound so that conversation becomes impossible. And to engage our sense of vision, there must be a television on to bring us the latest news, weather and sports, which we didn't ask to see but there it is invading our meal and giving us breaking information updates. Whose voice do you listen for? Lent is a time to listen for the one voice of the Living God. Twice in my youth, I remember hearing God's voice and twice I was saved from drowning. Both times I was being held underwater and struggling, but it was not helping me escape, to once again breathe fresh air. God's still small voice was there, but it was covered up by the sounds around me, including my own voice of fear.

"Obey my voice, and I will be your God, and you shall be my people..." says the Lord. Obedience. Sometimes our pets are more obedient than we are as Christians and they certainly help us understand the unconditional love that only comes from God. After we discern whether it is the spirit of the age or the Holy Spirit that we hear, we are then called to obedience. The Mother of our Lord was obedient, the apostles were obedient and all of the saints were obedient. Why is it so hard for us who believe to be obedient? Our baptismal covenant commits us to seek God's will and sacrifice daily to be one of His people. Walking our own way, doing our own thing and seeking what the world says is success is not what our Lord either demands or commands. Lord, help me to seek you in all things during this season of Lent whereby I may be drawn closer to you and love you more. Amen.

THE REV. CANON H.W. 'SANDY' HERRMANN, SSC, '89
Canon Herrmann is Rector of Church of Saint David of Wales in Denton, Texas. He currently serves as a Trustee on the Board at Nashotah House Theological Seminary. He and his wife, Ginger, have been married for over 30 years. They have two married daughters, Jamie married to Ben, living in Leander, Texas and Meredith married to John, living in Nashville, Tennessee.

LENTEN
MEDITATIONS

Meditation Twenty-Two

First Psalm: Psalm 119:97-120
Second Psalm: Psalm 81; Psalm 82
Old Testament: Jeremiah 8:18-9:6
New Testament: Romans 5:1-11
Gospel: John 8:12-20

My eyes are blind when I stand looking for something in the refrigerator. I will stand with the door open and the light shining brightly for 10 minutes looking for the mayonnaise. My wife will walk up behind me, and in two seconds take hold of the very thing I could not see. She says I have a mental block when it comes to anything that has to do with the kitchen, a mental block that keeps me from seeing what I need to see.

I cannot help but think the ancient Israelites had a similar problem. They stood in the very Light of God and were blind to it. Perhaps they too had a mental block, a mental block created by cultural expectation, personal fears, and legalism.

This is the second of Jesus' "I am" statements in the Gospel of John. Each statement is an attempt on the part of Jesus to reveal the nature of His Divinity. Using symbols familiar to both religious and common life: I am the Bread of Life; I am the Good Shepherd; I am the Light of the World, Jesus is saying that He Himself has come to fulfill both their religious and their human needs; He is the source of all true fulfillment.

The Pharisees respond by putting on their legalistic blinders. They say in essence, "We refuse to accept what you say because it doesn't fit into our legal framework." The Jewish Legal system required more than one witness to validate a testimony, and Jesus was making a claim without a witness. Their response would be akin to someone bringing food to starving people and the people saying, "Oh, sorry, we can't eat bread on Wednesdays because of what our legal system says."

Jesus tells them that He does have a witness, the only one capable of witnessing such a claim—God; but it wouldn't matter, as they have decided to see only from a human perspective ...you judge according to the flesh. They have a mental block: an inability or an unwillingness to see the very Light of God because of their own small- mindedness, their cultural shaping, their fears that hold onto an empty legalism.

I wonder if we are just as guilty as the ancient Israelites and Pharisees? How often does God seek to shine the Light of Christ into the darkness of our own wounds, or our wrongheadedness, and we are unable to see? Have we allowed ourselves to be so swallowed up by the thinking of a secular culture or so clouded by our own fears, that we simply do not see the very thing God has put before us?

THE REV. ERIC DUDLEY

Fr. Eric Dudley is rector of St. Peter's Anglican Church in Tallahassee Florida. St. Peter's is the Pro-Cathedral of the Gulf-Atlantic Diocese of the Anglican Church in North America. Fr. Dudley has degrees from Wofford (BA), Vanderbilt (M.Div.), and Yale (STM). A friend of Nashotah House, he is married to Belinda, and they have three children.

Meditation Twenty-Three

First Psalm: Psalm 83; Psalm 42; Psalm 43
Second Psalm: Psalm 85; Psalm 86
Old Testament: Jeremiah 10:11-24
New Testament: Romans 5:12-21
Gospel: John 8:21-32

What do we modern people really know about freedom? G.K. Chesterton reminds us that freedom, in the modern sense, is at root fear. "It is not so much that we are too bold to endure rules; it is that we are too timid to endure responsibilities." Our timidity is indeed masked by the fictional freedom of individual will, the will to be "who I am," the will to "do as I please," or the will to "speak my mind." These modern virtues of individualism, pervasive throughout American culture, hold fear at bay, but only for a time. Evading fear is the new self-mastery—the mastery of self-avoidance. It is the irony of individualism to seek freedom by avoiding the individual. We are passive aggressive toward ourselves.

By now, chances are that many of us have failed to endure the responsibilities of a holy Lent. Why? Because we are prone to treat Lent as avoidance—as a time of abstinence from the luxuries of a world on the verge of consuming itself. In our attempts to avoid the worldly we often fail to attend to what is holy. We think of fasting, for instance, as not eating. Fasting, however, is a matter of consuming less in order to give more to the hungry. Fasting is about satiating the hunger of others and becoming friends with those with whom we share our resources. Likewise, a Lenten discipline of prayer is not about a painful interruption into our daily schedules, so as to "make time for God." Prayer is nothing so terrible and humdrum as this. Rather, it is a continuous reorienting of our very posture. It is about learning the rhythm of life, wherein all our concerns are rightly perceived. Freedom comes from being responsible to the prayer of Christ, "Not my will, but thy will be done."

The free gift of God's grace is a binding freedom. It is an entering into Christ's redeeming act, an entering into the passion of him who does nothing on his own. As the Father is always with the Son because Christ always does what is pleasing to the Father, likewise is the Father always with us, not because we are so pleasing, but because we have been united to him who cannot but please the Father. This truth, however, will only set us free if we are responsible to it. Freedom in Christ is knowing that we cannot please God. We will know this freedom when the discipline of Christ has been inscribed upon our bodies through prayer and fasting. Through such habits we learn to inhabit our bodies more deeply. Hereby will we know what it means to dwell in Christ and for Christ to dwell in us.

THE REV. DR. WILLIAM O. DANIEL, JR., '12

The Rev. William O. Daniel, Jr., PhD, is Chaplain and Professor of Religion and Ethics in Saint James School, Hagerstown, Maryland, where he lives with his wife Amanda and their two children, Wyles and Aydah.

MEDITATION TWENTY-FOUR

FIRST PSALM: PSALM 95; PSALM 88
SECOND PSALM: PSALM 91; PSALM 92
OLD TESTAMENT: JEREMIAH 11:1-8; JEREMIAH 11:14-20
NEW TESTAMENT: ROMANS 6:1-11
GOSPEL: JOHN 8:33-47

"Whoever is of God hears the words of God," Jesus tells us (Jn. 8:47). Are we listening? Or are we like those who have become completely deaf to his call, whom Jesus calls children of the devil (Jn. 8:44)?

A vague faith in the Fatherhood of God is not enough. This even Jesus' opponents professed (Jn. 8:41). The presumption that God will gladly go on, bountiful and benevolent, in the face of our disobedience and disinterest is deadly: thus the Lord calls to us through the voice of the prophet, "Hear the words of the covenant!" (Jer. 11:2) Indeed, "hear the words of the covenant and do them" (Jer. 11:6).

Our complacency is an acid eating us from within, and an open foolishness provoking disaster from without. Let us turn. And listen. And do. "If today you hear his voice," calls the Psalmist, "harden not your hearts" (Ps. 95:7).

To commit sin is to be a slave to sin (Jn. 8:34). Of course, of our own we can do nothing. Of our own, we do not have the power to resist sin, much less overcome it. We have no power in ourselves to help ourselves. Yet if the Son sets you free, you will be free indeed (Jn. 8:36). Sharing in Christ's atoning death, we become dead to sin (Rom. 6:7-8). Sharing in His vivifying Resurrection, we rise up to walk with him in newness of life (Rom. 6:4). This is how we should consider ourselves as dead to sin, but alive to God in Christ Jesus (Rom. 6:11).

These words – if we listen to them – what do they say? What do they do? They are ancient truths, familiar truths. Have they become so familiar as to become falsehoods? Have we settled for an easy satisfaction, for the corruption of a comfortable coherence, and thus missed the Resurrection power of new life breaking in?

It is hard not to harden your heart against the word that comes to condemn you. It is hard not to steel yourself against the word that comes to kill you. Yet this season calls us to take the journey of death with our Lord. This is the time to dwell in the stinging side of Jesus' words, to allow him to confront us with our inadequacy, and remind us of the judgment we justly deserve for our want of obedience.

Of our own, we have no power to live the Resurrection life. But we can choose to embrace, rather than resist, the death that precedes it. We can choose to receive, rather than reject, the One who with his judgment brings it. And the promise, as we do so, is that we will share in his New Life when He comes to impart it.

THE REV. NATHANIEL KIDD, '12

The Rev. Nathaniel Kidd, '12, sojourns in the wilderness of PhD studies at Marquette University. He also teaches periodically at Lahore College of Theology in Lahore, Pakistan. He is grateful to God for his wife Sarah and baby daughter Madeleine who gladly endure with him the cold of Milwaukee and heat of Lahore as he daily seeks to serve and follow our Lord.

MEDITATION TWENTY-FIVE

FIRST PSALM: PSALM 87; PSALM 90
SECOND PSALM: PSALM 136
OLD TESTAMENT: JEREMIAH 13:1-11
NEW TESTAMENT: ROMANS 6:12-23
GOSPEL: JOHN 8:47-59

They picked up stones to throw at him (v.59). What? How can this be? Jesus' listeners want to stone him? But why? What could Jesus have said to make his listeners want to kill him?

We find the answer in John 8 where Jesus is in a ferocious discussion with the religious leaders in Jerusalem. He had claimed to be the light of the world (v.12), a not-so-veiled reference to being God, and then went on to teach: *If you abide in my word, you are truly my disciples, and you will know the truth, and the truth will set you free* (v.31f). The religious leaders respond by trying to discredit him claiming he was a Samaritan and had a demon! (v.48, 52). They understood that they were obviously holy and righteous because they were descendants of Abraham (v.33, 53). When Jesus responds that Abraham rejoiced to see his day, they just can't take it anymore thinking he is out of his mind (v.56).

As you read the narrative or listen to it read aloud, you can feel the intensity of the conversation growing, and then the climax when Jesus says to them, *Truly, Truly, I say to you, Before Abraham was, I am* (v.58). It is then that his listeners pick up stones to try to kill him. But why? Why does this provoke such a strong reaction?

It has everything to do with the words he used. He uses the Divine Name, the Name of God, which the Jews would never say, even when reading the Scriptures. Not only does Jesus say it (which they considered blasphemy), but he claims it for himself. In essence He is saying at that moment, *I am the Lord God. I am the Creator of heaven and earth. I am the One who spoke to Moses. I am the One who led Abraham, Isaac, and Jacob.*

Jesus is bringing all eternity-past into the present by speaking these words. Leon Morris, the Australian Anglican scholar writes: *It should also be observed that He says, "I am," not "I was." It is eternity of being and not simply being which has lasted through several centuries that the expression indicates.*[1] This is why the Apostle John begins his Gospel with *In the beginning was the Word, and the Word was with God, and the Word was God. He was in the beginning with God* (Jn. 1:1).

We affirm this every week in the Creed: *God from God, Light from Light, Very God of Very God.* We can hear it, read about it, and even preach it, but as William Temple observes *the apprehension of that truth must come through the response of men's souls.*[2] Picking up stones was their response. What is your response?

1. Leon Morris, *The Gospel According to John* (Grand Rapids, Mich.: Eerdmans, 1971), p. 474.

2. William Temple, *Readings in St. John's Gospel* (New York: Morehouse Publishing, 1985), p. 150.

THE MOST REV. DR. FOLEY BEACH

Dr. Beach is the Archbishop of the Anglican Church in North America (ACNA). Dr. Beach is a graduate of Gordon-Conwell Theological Seminary, the School of Theology at Sewanee, the University of the South, and Georgia State University. He has served in ministry with Young Life, the Episcopal Church, and the Anglican Church. Married for more than 30 years, he and his wife, Allison, have two grown children and make their home in the Atlanta, Georgia area.

Meditation Twenty-Six

FIRST PSALM: PSALM 66; PSALM 67
SECOND PSALM: PSALM 19; PSALM 46
OLD TESTAMENT: JEREMIAH 14:1-9; JEREMIAH 14:17-22
NEW TESTAMENT: GALATIANS 4:21-5:1
GOSPEL: MARK 8:11-21

The prophet paints a bleak portrait of Israel's state: servants and farmers despair for lack of water, the hind abandons her calf, the wild ass pants like a jackal and resigns itself to starvation. Far from being the innocent victim, however, Israel in her pride has followed false prophets and faithless priests into this lifeless desert. The literal death and disease Israel faces are merely the signs of the even greater desolation of their souls, "For both prophet and priest ply their trade through the land, and have no knowledge."

Though these prophets and priests have grievously wounded the Lord's virgin daughter Israel, at least one faithful prophet remains, and his inspired voice cries out in repentance, "We acknowledge our wickedness, O LORD, and the iniquity of our fathers, for we have sinned against thee. Do not spurn us, for thy name's sake; do not dishonor thy glorious throne; remember and do not break thy covenant with us."

I find it fascinating that by inflicting his people with a just punishment, God manages to get out of them the very cry he'd been looking for all along: a cry from the heart, acknowledging the covenant and calling out desperately for the realization of God's promises. Could it be God has foreseen all of this, and has Israel just where he wants her?

I suspect this is, in fact, the case, and our Gospel confirms it. Before the feeding of the four thousand, the disciples ask Jesus: "How can one feed these men with bread here in the desert?" (Mk. 8:4). How, indeed? Their question betrays them: they are either poorly-educated Jews who know nothing of the Exodus story, or they have no idea who Jesus is. I suspect it is the latter. Yet again the Lord has drawn his people into the desert for their edification, though this time he refuses to let Israel think man shall live by bread alone (Mt. 4). Hence his question, "Do you not yet understand?"

In a pleasing paradox, the Great Shepherd draws his people out into the desert that he might feed them with the bread of life, the bread from heaven (Jn. 6:31ff). In our epistle, we see that the woman who was fruitful in the end was Sara, the one who first was barren. In his supreme wisdom, the Holy Spirit brings the church year after year into the desert of Lent, that she might learn to be fruitful through her barrenness, and be made free through restriction and want. It seems we learn best in the desert, and when seen through the eyes of faith, in the arid soil of Lent we find the beginnings of genuine growth, and seek to find our perfection in the utter loss and glory of the Cross.

THE REV. JEREMY WILLIAM BERGSTROM, PHD (DURHAM, ENGLAND)
ANGLICAN STUDIES CERTIFICATE, NASHOTAH HOUSE, 2012
Fr. Bergstrom is husband to Jackie and the proud father of three wild and wonderful little boys: Nathanael, William, and Colman. He has been described as a "Patristic fundamentalist," and seeks the perfect balance of priestly ministry and scholarship in the service of Christ's church. Fr. Bergstrom serves as Priest Assistant, St. John's Church, Savannah and is Adjunct Professor in Historical and Ascetical Theology, Nashotah House.

MEDITATION TWENTY-SEVEN

FIRST PSALM: PSALM 89:1-18
SECOND PSALM: PSALM 89:19-52
OLD TESTAMENT: JEREMIAH 16:10-21
NEW TESTAMENT: ROMANS 7:1-12
GOSPEL: JOHN 6:1-15

Today's readings remind me of how I experience scarcity. When I become aware of fissures between who I think I am and who I desire to become, the gaps feel like cavities in my soul. But being reminded of my neediness exposes not just the poverty of those familiar chasms but also the emptiness of what I consider to be my achievements, particularly spiritual ones. When I taste this double-edged pinch, I feel cut off from God's steadfast love—because I believe it to be opposed to my scarcity. I realize I am actually asking, "When, O LORD, will I be satisfied? With my own faithfulness and holiness? With the life of the Church?" How profoundly I stand in want when I perceive scarcity as capable of blocking God's presence!

Scripture records how often the people of God view deficiency as antithetical to abundant life. Psalm 89 begins by praising God for providing through dramatic interventions, identifying political triumph as a gift from the One whose throne stands upon all good things: righteousness, justice, and faithfulness. Yet the same poem ends in a whimper of desperate need stemming from the acknowledgment of sinful disobedience: "How long, O LORD? Will you hide yourself forever? Remember how short my time is… Where is your steadfast love of old?" Receiving God's abundance often appears at risk of being occluded by our faithlessness, our shortcomings, our failure.

What happens when we perceive, as in the rest of this Psalm and Jeremiah 16, that God's steadfast love remains present and operative in the places where we experience ourselves or others as failing or as under judgment? When we receive the faithfulness of the Father resting upon places we know as insufficient, not despite their deficiencies, but within them? When we realize that even what we thought we possessed pales next to the love of God in Christ, and that what we consider lacking has already been made up and surpassed, so much so that there are leftovers spilling out of the baskets of our lives?

We are surrounded by the God whose redemption arcs alongside, within, and underneath his judgments and who surely brings us to his own land of plenty—that home where nothing is lost, where even fragments of righteousness are gathered up, where our hunger encounters God's steadfast love and disappears into his abundance. Here, both our lack and the things we view as accomplishments are transfigured such that they become vessels of the love of God. And we are satisfied, replete even, in the lavishness of the Trinity.

KIRSTEN LAUREL GUIDERO

Kirsten Laurel Guidero gladly crosses paths with graduates and faculty of the House and has benefited from several of its symposia. A doctoral candidate in theology, pastor, and postulant to ordained ministry, Kirsten lives in Milwaukee, Wisconsin with her husband, Darin Fawley (a doctoral candidate in theology & philosophy and middle school history teacher), and their rescue dog, Lucy. Her passion is to help people identify and respond more deeply to the presence of God in their lives, whether that is through grappling with Scripture and theology, learning habits of discipleship, inhabiting the church seasons, engaging with the world around us, or entering into contemplative prayer.

MEDITATION TWENTY-EIGHT

First Psalm: Psalm 97; Psalm 99; Psalm 100
Second Psalm: Psalm 94; Psalm 95
Old Testament: Jeremiah 17:19-27
New Testament: Romans 7:13-25
Gospel: John 6:16-27

Commenting on his life before he came to know the Messiah, Paul speaks of sin in a way that echoes the tragic events of Genesis 3:1-24. Sin took the opportunity afforded by the commandment and deceived Adam and Eve. The word Paul uses for deception is the same word Eve used when recounting her encounter with the serpent: "Then the LORD God said to the woman, 'What is this you have done?' The woman said, The serpent deceived me, and I ate (Gen. 3:13)."

By connecting Eve's first encounter with sin to his own, Paul makes a startlingly perceptive statement about sin and the human experience. Sin is both destructive and dishonest. The serpent offered Adam and Eve the opportunity to achieve divinity. Instead they came to know alienation from God and each other.

Paul claims that the experience of sin promising what it cannot provide is universal. Is he correct? Do we experience moments when the promises of sin and the desires of our eyes (Gen. 3:6) lead us to believe that life might be a little better with more sin and less God? Did we then have our eyes opened to see the havoc and disillusionment that inevitably follows? Paul's query towards the end of this chapter has a ring of universality as well, "Who will rescue me?" (Rom. 7:24). Paul knows the answer. Jesus has already freed us.

The interior struggle and sense of defeat in Romans 7 gives way to the proclamation of victory in Romans 8:1-2: "Therefore, there is now no condemnation for those who are in Christ Jesus, because through Christ Jesus the law of the Spirit who gives life has set you free from the law of sin and death."

Sin has been defeated, but a defeated enemy still has the ability to lie. The church, in its wisdom, has given us the season of Lent as an opportunity to reflect upon this very reality. Are there lies — spurred on by our own desires — that we have once again begun to believe? Are we relying on God's Spirit, His scriptures, and the sacraments to give us the ability to discern and dismiss the lies that sin tells us? Sin lied to us, we ate, and found ourselves aching to be satisfied. During Lent we fast, remind ourselves of the truth, and are filled with God's pleasure.

THE REV. ESAU MCCAULLEY

The Rev. Esau McCaulley received his Masters in Sacred Theology (STM) in 2013 from Nashotah House. He is a priest in the Diocese of Albany, husband to Mandy, father to Luke, Clare, and Peter. Currently, he is a doctoral candidate in New Testament at the University of St. Andrews studying under the supervision of N.T. Wright.

LENTEN
MEDITATIONS

Meditation Twenty-Nine

First Psalm: Psalm 101; Psalm 109:1-4;
Psalm 109:5-19; Psalm 109:20-30
Second Psalm: Psalm 119:121-144
Old Testament: Jeremiah 18:1-11
New Testament: Romans 8:1-11
Gospel: John 6:27-40

"Everything that the Father gives me will come to me, and anyone who comes to me I will never drive away; for I have come down from heaven, not to do my own will, but the will of him who sent me, that I should lose nothing of all that he has given me, but raise it up on the last day." John 6:37-39

What must we do this Lent, to fulfill what God wants us to do? Jesus answers this question for us: "God wants you to believe in me. I am the one God has sent to you. God gave you to me, and I am charged with bringing you back to him." Jesus says to each one of us, "God told me not to lose you, because you are so very precious to him. No matter who you are, no matter what you have done, no matter what you think, no matter how you feel, I want to bring you back to him, because I love my father; therefore I long with all my heart to do the task he has given me. So come to me and believe in me. Because I love my father with all my being, so do I love you."

Do you see that Jesus doesn't tell us here to have faith, or to love anybody, or to think or to be anything more than or other than what we are right now? He just says, "Believe me. This is the only thing God asks of you. This is how you do God's work, how you follow God's will." And how do we show Jesus that we believe? Simply by coming to him when he calls us. We are called to follow our Beloved, just as the first disciples were called: "Come. Follow me." They dropped everything and followed him.

Our first step in following the will of God, you see, is an act of obedience. The journey of Lent is a journey of following our Lord. You would think it would be simple; just as sheep hear their shepherd's voice and follow him, so would we hearken to our Shepherd's voice and follow him. But we don't. We are afraid. We think it's going to hurt. Though we yearn to fall into his arms and be comforted, we face the most basic of all fears—the fear of annihilation. This fear turns our hearts cold. We try to reason about it, to imagine, to intellectualize, to reassure ourselves. But not one of these works. This is why Jesus told us to be like little children. You know how they fling themselves with complete self-abandonment into the arms (or kneecaps!) of the adults they love and trust. And you know how we catch them up into our arms, embracing them, enfolding them into our very hearts. And you know how good it makes both you and the child feel to hold and to be held, heart to heart. All time ceases, all space disappears, until there is nothing else but Love.

THE REV. CAROLYN BALLINGER, PH.D.

Mother Carolyn is connected to Nashotah House because she took one class during the summer of 2014, and somehow left a part of herself there and took a part of the House home with her. She is a "circuit-rider" in the Diocese of Western Kansas, going out wherever her Bishop sends her to serve in places that otherwise have no priest. She has two sons, Rick and Ned, two lovely daughters-in-law, Laurel and Michelle, three grandchildren, Jasmine, Eddie, and Neva, dozens of cousins, and some dearest of friends.

Meditation Thirty

FIRST PSALM: PSALM 69:1-23; PSALM 69:24-30;
PSALM 69:31-36
SECOND PSALM: PSALM 73
OLD TESTAMENT: JEREMIAH 22:13-23
NEW TESTAMENT: ROMANS 8:12-27
GOSPEL: JOHN 6:41-51

Many cultural historians have argued and agreed that Americans in the twenty-first century are far busier than any other time in our nation's history. Considering the technological, medical, and scientific advances we have made, this should not be surprising to anyone. The amount of time it has taken us to advance in the aforementioned areas is nothing short of astonishing.

As much a blessing it is to continue to grow and prosper, there is a downside. The downside is the reliance on our human intellectual base. It takes an incredible amount of intellect to advance at the rate in which we have. However, this reliance on our human intellect causes us to be blind to the vision and the deaf to the voice of God.

In the Gospel text, the members of Jesus' community are using their human intellect to question "the son of Joseph, whom they all know." They have dismissed him because he did not pass their test based upon their human intellect. They know who he is from their community and believe that he cannot possibly be the Son of God.

Unfortunately, we do this exact same thing. We dismiss complex situations in our communities, in our states and in the world based upon our limited understanding. At the time of this writing, there have been a series of incidents nationwide involving those who are of different racial groups. The temptation, based upon our human intellect, is to either dismiss the role of race, or describe the event as an issue only of race. Both are based solely on our human intellect. So-called pundits and experts use various sources of data to defend their perspective. Due to our extreme busyness, we take what they present, accept it as our own, and expand our human intellectual base.

The question that we, and the Jewish community of Jesus failed to ask is, "Where is God in this?" Due to our reliance on our own understanding, we indirectly push God out of the equation. We close our eyes to shield us from what he wants us to see. We put our fingers in our ears to deafen ourselves to his voice. In doing so, we are not only separating ourselves from him, but from each other.

During this Lenten period, reflect on a strained relationship or an issue you are passionate about. Ask God to show you the perspective of the other. Ask him to give you the strength and desire to rely on him, his vision, his words. May his grace shine upon you, and grant you peace.

THE REV. JAMES M. HAIRSTON, FSAC
DMIN STUDENT, NASHOTAH HOUSE THEOLOGICAL SEMINARY,'16
The Rev. James Hairston serves as Assistant Vicar of the Anglican Church of the Redeemer (ACNA), Norwood, MA. As a Chaplain in the United States Army, he was deployed in support of Operation Enduring Freedom in Afghanistan. Fr. Hairston is also a teacher and counselor at the local county prison. Married to Elizabeth, they are the proud parents of son, Jay.

MEDITATION THIRTY-ONE

FIRST PSALM: PSALM 95; PSALM 102
SECOND PSALM: PSALM 107:1-32
OLD TESTAMENT: JEREMIAH 23:1-8
NEW TESTAMENT: ROMANS 8:28-39
GOSPEL: JOHN 6:52-59

Chapters 9-11 in *The Rule of St. Benedict* directs how the Night Office is to be said (much of which is reflected in the Prayer Book service of Matins). Whether in winter or in summer, the office begins in the same way: a three-fold repetition, Lord, open thou our lips/ And our mouth shall shew forth thy praise, followed by Psalm 95, the Venite. One of the most grievous losses in the American Prayer Book tradition is the loss of the end of verse 7, and verses 8-11 of the psalm, replacing them with verses 9 and 13 of Psalm 96 (wonderfully, however, the 1979 BCP restores the end of verse 7 in the Rite II service [Oh, that today you would harken to his voice!] and also provides the full psalm in Coverdale's translation on page 146 to use instead).

Today if ye will hear his voice, harden not your hearts
  as in the provocation,
  and as in the day of temptation in the wilderness;
When your fathers tempted me,
  proved me, and saw my works.
Forty years long was I grieved with this generation, and said,
  It is a people that do err in their hearts,
  for they have not known my ways.
Unto whom I sware in my wrath,
  that they should not enter into my rest.

The epistle to the Hebrews presents an exegetical sermon on Psalm 95 in chapters 3 and 4. The first chapter opens with a luminous description of the coming of Jesus, while the second half weaves Old Testament passages to buttress the argument. "Therefore," chapter 2 begins, "we must pay the closer attention to what we have heard, lest we drift away from it." Jesus is an apostle, a great high priest (3:1) and interestingly, "the builder of a house" (3:3). "We are his house," the sermon explains, "if we hold fast our confidence" (3:6). The warning from the Holy Spirit (3:7) at the end of Psalm 95 is quoted in its entirety in order that we might "take care … lest there be in any of you an evil and unbelieving heart, leading you to fall away from the living God" (3:12).

St. Benedict reflects what is clearly a tradition that predates him that thought that a meditation on the profound similitude between Israel's rebellion and my own heart is how the Christian should begin each day. We "strive to enter" (4:11) the "Sabbath rest [that remains] for the people of God" (4:9) by true repentance (3:13-18), by seeking after the divine gift of Faith (3:19-4:4) and by means of the Word of God (4:12) whom we encounter in sacred scripture and the sacraments. Our confidence and hope rests only on Jesus, for "He can deal gently with the ignorant and wayward, since he himself is beset with weakness" (5:2). To pray Psalm 95 in earnest is to find ourselves united to the eternal Victim who offers himself as our Great High Priest. There is life.

THE REV. MATTHEW S C OLVER

Fr. Olver is the Teaching Fellow in Liturgics at Nashotah House Theological Seminary and a doctoral student at Marquette University. Before coming to Milwaukee, he was for seven years the Assistant Rector at Church of the Incarnation, Dallas and undertook his previous studies at Wheaton College and Duke Divinity School. He is married to Kristen and they have two elementary-aged children, Claire and Isaac. He has been a member of the Anglican-Roman Catholic Consultation in the U.S. (ARCUSA) since 2006.

Meditation Thirty-Two

First Psalm: Psalm 107:33-43; Psalm 108:1-6;
Psalm 108:7-13
Second Psalm: Psalm 33
Old Testament: Jeremiah 23:9-15
New Testament: Romans 9:1-18
Gospel: John 6:60-71

"It is the Spirit who gives life; the flesh profits nothing; the words that I have spoken to you are spirit and are life." Wait. Jesus was just teaching, "I am the bread of life" and "my flesh is real food, my blood real drink." What is he saying?

Firstly, let us remember that throughout John's Gospel matter is "spirit-bearing." The Incarnation—the Word becoming flesh—is our preeminent example. Cyril of Alexandria reflected: "It is not the nature of the flesh that renders the Spirit life-giving but the might of the spirit that makes the body life-giving...he says that the flesh can profit nothing...insofar as it is mere human flesh. But when flesh is understood and believed to be the temple of the Word...it will be a channel of sanctification and life, not altogether of itself but through God who has been made one with it...."

Hmm.... Let's assume for a moment that we remain puzzled, perhaps even defensive, like those who first heard Jesus' words. His questions are rather like corkscrews, after all; they make their way down into the depths, drawing out hearts. And he doesn't even apologize! "Does my teaching offend you? What if you see the Son of Man ascend to where he was before?" This ascent (in the light of Jn 3.14) began on the horribly offensive instrument of Roman execution. Jesus is intimating, "If this offends you, the offense is only going to get worse!"

So why did the Twelve stay? They probably didn't understand Jesus' teaching any better than the deserters. Peter's response helps us: they understood Jesus to be the Holy One of God. However partial their understanding, they were convinced he was of God, and his words, words of life.

At this stage in Lent, you may be discovering that the Lord is asking you a question. Or challenging you in unexpected ways. Perhaps he is revealing something about himself, or indicating a reality about yourself, that you would rather not face. Today, you know more about who Jesus of Nazareth is than the Twelve did in John 6. You know that he has given himself up for love of you, to bring you into union with himself, and to gift you with the Kingdom.

So cling to him with all your might, in the midst of your desire to avoid, escape, squirrel out from under, or justify yourself. Find a way to express how you are feeling to the Lord. Welcome the Holy Spirit (more—beg him to come) into your dark places. And be comforted: the One who is the Truth will set you free.

1. Rodney A. Whitaker, *John, The IVP New Testament Commentary, Series 4* (Downers Grove, Ill.: InterVarsity Press, 1999), 152; 163.

2. Cyril of Alexandria, *Commentary on John, in: Elowsky, Joel C., ed. John 1-10, Ancient Christian Commentary on Scripture* (Downers Grove, Ill.: InterVarsity Press, 2006), 246.

ARDATH L. SMITH

Ardath L. Smith will be graduating with an MDiv from Nashotah House in May 2015. She has served since 2001 with Church Resource Ministries on their Staff Development and Care Team, providing pastoral care and spiritual direction to missionaries within, and beyond, CRM. She is discerning, with her sister Renée Smith and several others, a call to form a community in Northern Wales whose members are called to prayer and ministry to missionaries.

MEDITATION THIRTY-THREE

FIRST PSALM: PSALM 118
SECOND PSALM: PSALM 145
OLD TESTAMENT: JEREMIAH 23:16–32
NEW TESTAMENT: 1 CORINTHIANS 9:19–27
GOSPEL: MARK 8:31–9:1

Jeremiah is often called "the weeping prophet." In a famous painting of 1630, Rembrandt conveyed this image: the prophet sits in the dark with his head in his hand, his eyes downcast, his brow furrowed with grief. The city of Jerusalem burns in the background. Because the early chapters of the book are saturated with lament, the Daily Office Lectionary makes heavy use of Jeremiah during Lent in Year One. In this season, we mourn the devastation that sin has caused.

If, however, we think of Jeremiah only as "the weeping prophet," we run the risk of misunderstanding him. He did cry at times (9:1), but he was never a weak victim. Rather, Jeremiah was the Rambo of Israel's prophets. In the 1980s, Sylvester Stallone starred in a series of action movies as John Rambo, a Vietnam veteran who had suffered profoundly but remained amazingly tough and resourceful. He was always reluctant to fight, but when drawn into the fray, he tied on his headband and became a one-man army. Jeremiah was a reluctant prophet (1:1–10), but God clothed him for action and armed him with divine words "to pluck up and to break down, to destroy and overthrow" (v. 10). He faced impossible odds, taking on the entire nation of Judah and many foreign nations. He labored virtually alone for over forty years.

Today's Old Testament reading is part of a larger passage (23:9–40) in which God, through Jeremiah, attacks an army of false prophets.

False prophets can be recognized by their immoral lifestyles. Their actions cast doubt on their words. In addition, their message is all sweetness and light: "It shall be well with you" (v. 17). They tell people what they want to hear, but they never deliver a hard word to turn their hearers from sin. They proclaim their own visions and dreams. They lack divine authority because they have not stood in God's council, and their teachings contradict what God has already spoken.

Like Jeremiah, our Lord Jesus Christ warned his followers to be on guard against false prophets who bear bad fruit (Matt 7:15). He also predicted that numerous false prophets would arise in the future to lead many astray (24:11). This Lent, we need to realize that we are in a spiritual battle with stylish and seductive falsehoods. The odds seem to be against us, but we must not sit and weep. We are not alone; God himself is with us. We do not take up human weapons in this fight. Rather, we take up the powerful word of God: "Is not my word like fire, declares the LORD, and like a hammer that breaks the rock in pieces?" (Jer 23:29).

TRAVIS BOTT, PHD
ASSISTANT PROFESSOR OF OLD TESTAMENT AND HEBREW
NASHOTAH HOUSE THEOLOGICAL SEMINARY

Dr. Bott grew up in a small logging town in the beautifully rainy Pacific Northwest. In college, he naively attempted to master the Bible in one year. He began teaching himself Hebrew at night while working as a house painter by day. Through many years of study, he has learned to appreciate both the depth of Scripture and the shallowness of his own understanding. He now regards himself as a lifelong servant of the Word. Travis and his wife, Jill, have two sons, Stephen and Peter, and a daughter, Elizabeth.

MEDITATION THIRTY-FOUR

FIRST PSALM: PSALM 31
SECOND PSALM: PSALM 35
OLD TESTAMENT: JEREMIAH 24
NEW TESTAMENT: ROMANS 9:19-33
GOSPEL: JOHN 9:1-17

Stood at the back of the crowded church, I wiped away the tears which ran down my face, as together we said goodbye to Jez. He had been 23, an active sportsman, a new teacher with a promising career, a dear friend. The emergency surgery to remove an undiagnosed brain tumor had been unsuccessful and I watched, emotionally numb, as his mother spoke of her beautiful boy and others paid tribute to the man who was now gone from amongst us. Why God, why HIM?

There are times in our lives when our natural response to events is to question God, to blame Him, to lose faith, and yet it seems as though today's reading from Romans reprimands those who would question God. Who are we, mere humans, to challenge the divine freedom of God to deal with those He has created in whichever way he chooses? Paul makes a simple point; our concepts of good and bad, fair and corrupt are not the same as God's understanding, nor the outworking of His good purposes.

Faced with questions and difficult circumstances, there are those who will simply say that to question God is to forget that "all things work together for good for those who love God" (Rom.. 8:28), 'we may feel suffering now, but later good will come'. And whilst that is true to an extent, seeing this promise as temporal creates an image of God as divine mathematician, weighing up our sufferings and converting them to rewards, nice feelings or experiences. All of this leaves little hope for those who live entire lives of suffering; how does God turn the suffering of the famine struck, the terminally ill or the perpetual addict into good that can be seen?

What if we look beyond the worldly and human timescale, to the outlook of God? The goodness of God no longer looks like an instant healing, or a new car, or deliverance from a tough situation. God's goodness now looks like a man, beaten and bruised, bearing the weight of our sin for the sake of love. It looks a pile of grave clothes and an empty tomb and the amazement of those who saw Him in resurrection glory. God's goodness is best seen in the face of His son, our savior. He is savior not just of those of the old covenant, but as Paul explains, God now calls Gentiles 'my people'. All people are able to claim their place in the kingdom of the new covenant in His infinite love and grace.

When we question God then, as we inevitably will, we do so knowing that He has gathered all things together in His son, who is the true source of Goodness, and the one who enables us to see goodness and bring about true good for His sake.

Mr. Jamie Gater

Mr. Gater was pleased to visit Nashotah House during the Michaelmas 2014 term. He is a postulant for holy orders in the Church of England and currently finishing his studies at St Stephens House, Oxford, a covenant partner of Nashotah House. He and his wife Naomi have one son named Jonah.

MEDITATION THIRTY-FIVE

First Psalm: Psalm 120; Psalm 121; Psalm 122; Psalm 123
Second Psalm: Psalm 124; Psalm 125; Psalm 126; Psalm 127
Old Testament: Jeremiah 25:8-17
New Testament: Romans 10:1-13
Gospel: John 9:18-41

Blindness and sight, misperception and understanding: themes of judgment pervade the story of Jesus' healing of the man born blind. He first comes to our attention through the question of the disciples. A physical deficiency so profound demands a judgment, an accounting for it. "Who sinned? This man or his parents?"

Jesus' answer—Jesus' judgment—comes as a surprise: "Neither this man nor his parents sinned; he was born blind so that God's works might be revealed in him."

The problem Jesus exposes is a common one. It is produced by the assumption that the condition of the world and the problems and evils and hardships within it can be meaningfully understood, meaningfully judged, apart from the God who creates and redeems and sanctifies. But if you want an answer to how something so bad could make sense, you won't find one—unless you look for it in the light of the God whose judgment loves and heals and saves. If there is any hope of understanding the suffering, the pain, the confusion, the loss, the evils of the world, it is only to be found in the light of the same merciful judgment of God that takes the sinless Son of God to death on the cross for the sins of the world.

The disciples looked at a man born blind and arrived at the judgment that someone must have sinned terribly. The man's

FROM DUST TO TRIUMPH: REFLECTIONS FOR A HOLY LENT

neighbors looked at him, and their judgment was mixed: healed by Jesus, some of them saw him and some of them did not. The Pharisees looked at the man and arrived at the judgment that Jesus had done something wrong. Looking at God's merciful and saving judgment, all they saw was sin.

God's judgment cuts two ways. If we don't learn to see the world in the light of Jesus, if we don't perceive the judgment that he passes between good and evil by his words and deeds, then we, too, will go on stumbling through the darkness of our own blinded hearts.

But if we do learn to see as Jesus teaches and empowers us to see; if we pray for the Spirit's gifts of wisdom and understanding; if we offer our hearts and minds and hands to the Father's luminous will—that it might be done on earth as it is in heaven, in us as it was in the man born blind—then we, too, with eyes no longer blind, will live in the light of Christ.

THE REV. THOMAS N. BUCHAN III, PHD
ASSOCIATE PROFESSOR OF CHURCH HISTORY AT NASHOTAH HOUSE
AND PRIEST-IN-CHARGE AT ST. ANSKAR'S EPISCOPAL CHURCH,
HARTLAND, WISCONSIN

Fr. Buchan's academic interests include historiography, ancient Christian martyrdom and asceticism, the history of doctrines and practices of sanctification and holiness, Trinitarian theology, Christology, and the history of exegesis. He has published essays on biblical authority, "theosis" in Ephrem the Syrian, and the historical-theological method of John Wesley. Fr. Buchan and his wife, Shelly, have two children. As a family, they enjoy hiking, biking, reading, and their dog, Trixie.

LENTEN
MEDITATIONS

MEDITATION THIRTY-SIX

FIRST PSALM: PSALM 119:145-176
SECOND PSALM: PSALM 128; PSALM 129; PSALM 130
OLD TESTAMENT: JEREMIAH 25:30-38
NEW TESTAMENT: ROMANS 10:14-21
GOSPEL: JOHN 10:1-18

Last summer while visiting a friend in Oxfordshire we went on a long walk in the grounds of nearby Blenheim Palace traversing many fields that had been laid over to sheep pasture. As we walked and talked, paying little attention to the sheep, they continued to graze until we were within a few feet at which point they would scurry away bleating anxiously. In one field I decided to try to approach a group very slowly, making what I considered to be friendly noises as I inched forward. They were not impressed. On the contrary my attempts were met with even louder and more frantic bleating as they retreated as fast as their wool-laden bodies allowed, eyeing me with alarm until we had moved on to the next field.

A very different picture was presented in the BBC production An Island Parish filmed on the tiny island of Sark in the Channel Islands. Shepherd Dave's sheep followed as he called each by name. I couldn't tell them apart, but Dave could, and he pointed each one out to the presenter who quite evidently was having the same trouble I was in telling them apart. It was a hard life, especially in lambing season when he was out in all weather and at all times of the day and night helping the ewes to lamb, but they were his sheep, he owned them, and he cared for them.

Not so with Israel's shepherds at the time of Jeremiah. They had duped the sheep into trusting and following them. But they weren't the owners, just the hired hands, and they had led the owner's sheep into dangerous paths for which they were to be punished. Rescue came for the lost sheep of Israel, however, when the owner himself came and called them each by name, and not them only but other sheep also belonging to the owner. Safety would be found within the enclosure whose gate was the very body of the owner/shepherd himself, who placed himself between the wild ravenous beasts who were their enemy and the green pastures where they would be free from the fear of death.

This Good Shepherd knows your name: "he calls his own sheep by name." He knows intimately all the contours of your being: each hurt, each fear, each resentment, each joy, all of your past and all of your present, and he has come that you might have life and have it abundantly. He lays down his life to give you the fullness of life whose entrance is only through his body, for Jesus promised, "whoever enters by me will be saved."

THE REV. SARAH L. BRONOS, '07
The Rev. Sarah L. Bronos received her MDiv from Nashotah House in 2007 and has been the Rector of The Episcopal Church of the Good Shepherd in Maitland, Florida (Diocese of Central Florida) since 2009.

Meditation Thirty-Seven

FIRST PSALM: PSALM 131; PSALM 132; PSALM 133
SECOND PSALM: PSALM 140; PSALM 142
OLD TESTAMENT: JEREMIAH 26:1-16
NEW TESTAMENT: ROMANS 11:1-12
GOSPEL: JOHN 10:19-42

In the Daily Office lessons for today, we read of Jeremiah's ministerial experience, and Paul writes of Elijah's perspective on ministry. Both are speaking of the dangers of preaching to a hostile people who, perhaps even in their own minds, were failures. It may be that the only thing worse than being a failure is having someone else point out to us that we have failed. Let us face a ministerial reality, life rarely turns out well for God's prophets.

Jeremiah is sent to a hostile people to preach God's message of repentance. In Jeremiah's own prophecy, he records the mocking jeers of those who hated him: "For whenever I speak, I cry out, I shout, 'Violence and destruction!' For the word of the Lord has become to a reproach and a derision all the day long...for I hear many whispering, Denounce him, let us denounce him!' So say all my familiar friends, watching for my fall" (Jer. 20:8, 10). Jeremiah is being hounded, even by his friends, for speaking a word against them on behalf of God. Still, he carries on.

In today's Old Testament lection at Morning Prayer, God sends Jeremiah into Judah, and not only into Judah, but particularly into the temple. Imagine for a moment someone in the parish, a total stranger, who suddenly decides to preach at the front door of your church this Sunday. How might you react? Jeremiah stands in the court of the temple and preaches to all who come in as God instructs him: "Speak to all the who come to worship in the house of the LORD all the words that I command you to speak to them; do not hold back a word. It may be that they will listen, and every man turn from his evil way, that I may repent of the evil which I intend to do to them because of their evil doings." (Jer. 26:2-3)

There are many reasons to fear the audience as a preacher, particularly in the heavily politically-correct environment of today. Somehow, it has become almost a taboo to preach repentance, even in the Church. Some laity are tremendously supportive of the preacher—others, perhaps not as much. It can be quite tempting to pull our punches when it comes to preaching repentance during Lent. We fear beating them up so bad that they never return. There is a heavy temptation toward preaching more "almost Easter" sermons rather than Lenten themes of discipline, fasting, holiness, simplicity, or self-denial. But focus again, for a moment, on these words: "Do not hold back! It may be that they will listen, and every man turn from his evil way."

What would God have you preach to his people who are more frequently in a state of failure than success? Do not hold back. It may be that they will listen and repent.

THE REV. DR. JON C. JENKINS, 2006 (MDIV), AND 2013 (DMIN)
Fr. Jenkins is a professor of Bible and Ascetical Theology in various Catholic and Anglican programs, and serves as Associate Rector of All Saints Anglican Church in Peachtree City, Georgia in the Anglican Diocese of the South under the pastoral leadership of Archbishop Foley Beach. He and his wife Claire reside on the western perimeter of Atlanta, Georgia.

Meditation Thirty-Eight

First Psalm: Psalm 95; Psalm 22
Second Psalm: Psalm 141; Psalm 143:1-11; Psalm 143:12
Old Testament: Jeremiah 29:1; Jeremiah 29:4-13
New Testament: Romans 11:13-24
Gospel: John 11:1-27; John 12:1-10

"Do you believe this?"

Reflection on the words of John 11 often centers on the larger narrative of Lazarus or on the wonderful "I am" statement. Yet as we sit on the cusp of Holy Week, on the brink of our Lord's Passion, the question posed to Martha in verse 26 cuts to the heart of the matter. "Do you believe this?"

The question is one with wide ranging consequences. In this season it calls to mind the Lenten preparation we have been observing, and it flashes Holy Week before our eyes. For weeks we have been fasting and praying, seeking the will of God with an ever deepening fervor. One short week from now we will hear the words "It is finished" as the tension between life and death will come to a crescendo that culminates in silence and a tomb. But not yet. Before we finish Lent, before we reach Easter or Good Friday, we stop in front of another tomb. Lazarus is dead.

Today we wait to see what the Lord will do. We wait to see what hope there may still be. We wait now, just as we will wait in seven days' time. And though in both cases we know the story, it is not for us to rush through it. We must walk with the Lord. We must wait on the Lord. In the midst of waiting, the Lord offers those oh so familiar words, "I am…" Those comfortable words as we stand before Lazarus' tomb. Reassuring words as we draw ever nearer to that for which we have prepared.

But there is more. There is a question that remains before us just as it was asked of Martha. "Do you believe this?" It is this question that sets the final stage for all that upon which we are about to embark. It asks us to reflect on the Lent which we have observed. It asks us to wait when hope seems to run out. It asks us to decide, do we really believe all of this? Is Jesus who he says he is?

I invite us to pause today and ponder this. If he is, then there is more than a tomb for Lazarus. If he is, then our Lenten preparations are not in vain but draw us deeper into the mystery we are about to enter. If he is, then there is still more to come when we finally hear him say, "It is finished."

Jesus is who he says he is. Jesus is I am, the Christ, the Son of God, he who is coming into the world.

Do you believe this?

THE REV. BENJAMIN D. HANKINSON, JR. '14
The Rev. Ben Hankinson serves as Priest-in-Charge at Trinity Episcopal Church in Mt. Vernon, Illinois. Fr. Hankinson seeks to model his ministry around the Acts 2 church while encouraging the faithful to live out the Great Commission.

Meditation Thirty-Nine

First Psalm: Psalm 137:1-6; Psalm 137:7-9; Psalm 144
Second Psalm: Psalm 42; Psalm 43
Old Testament: Jeremiah 31:27-34
New Testament: Romans 11:25-36
Gospel: John 11:28-44; John 12:37-50

It is the day before Palm Sunday, the beginning of Holy Week. The Gospel appointed for this day is the raising of Lazarus from the dead. Not only is this the greatest miracle performed by Jesus, but also the raising of Lazarus is a foreshadowing of our Lord's own resurrection from the dead. That will be the greatest miracle for all time, for Lazarus would one day die again, but Jesus would be raised everlastingly, and his resurrection would be a sign that sin and death had been conquered once for all humanity on the cross.

Jesus' miracles were signs of his nature and his mission. Thus, his first miracle, the changing of water to wine, was a sign that he was the long-awaited Messiah and that the Messianic Age was beginning. Likewise, the raising of Lazarus, that miracle being Jesus' last before his passion and death, was a sign far beyond simply raising someone from the dead, as important as that was. Through this miracle he seems to be saying, "Pay attention. Witness what I am doing and remember it in the context of what I will soon endure in my passion and death."

A stronger sign of Jesus' nature had never been given. He had given sight to a man born blind, healed a paralytic, and even raised the dead; Lazarus, however, had been dead for four whole days. Jesus' identity was surely manifest to his friends and enemies alike. The miracle, rather than turning the hearts of those who were against him, merely solidified their resolve. Caiaphas, knowing that the raising of Lazarus would make it difficult, if not impossible, to disprove Jesus' Messianic identity, resolved to have Jesus put to death. It was in response to this miracle that Caiaphas uttered his prophetic phrase, "It is expedient that one man should die for the people, and that the whole nation perish not." On the other hand, for those who put their trust in Jesus, the raising of Lazarus solidified their faith and planted the seed of hope which would emerge after Jesus' resurrection.

As was the case with the miracle of the raising of Lazarus, our Lord's passion, death, and resurrection, as central as they are to the Christian faith, elicit a variety of responses: denial, hatred, trust, acceptance, devotion, etc. May God grant us the grace to respond anew this Holy Week and Easter with acceptance, trust, and love, that we may be brought ever closer to the God who loves us so much that "he gave his only begotten Son, to the end that all who believe in him should not perish, but have everlasting life."

THE VERY REV. FREDRICK A. ROBINSON, '82

The Very Rev. Fredrick A. Robinson is Rector of The Church of the Redeemer in the Diocese of Southwest Florida and a member of the Board of Trustees of Nashotah House Theological Seminary.

MEDITATION FORTY

FIRST PSALM: PSALM 24; PSALM 29
SECOND PSALM: PSALM 103
OLD TESTAMENT: ZECHARIAH 9:9-12; ZECHARIAH 12:9-11;
ZECHARIAH 13:1; ZECHARIAH 13:7-9
NEW TESTAMENT: 1 TIMOTHY 6:12-16
GOSPEL: MATTHEW 21:12-17

Today is Palm Sunday—the beginning of Holy Week. In the gospel lesson today, Jesus gives us a wonderful demonstration of how we should treat this sacred time. Matthew chapter 21 states: "Jesus entered the temple and drove out all who sold and bought in the temple, and he overturned the tables of the money-changers and the seats of those who sold pigeons. He said to them, "It is written, 'My house shall be called a house of prayer,' but you make it a den of robbers."

The first thing that Jesus does when entering Jerusalem to the accolades of the people is not to focus on them, but to direct his focus upon God the Father. Jesus heads directly to his Father's house to worship. So, too, we should not be distracted by the concerns of the world around us, not even the accolades of family or friends. Like Jesus, spending quality time with our Heavenly Father, in His house, should be a matter of the first order for us. Let us renew that fervor this Holy Week.

Secondly, Jesus recognizes the distractions and potential idols that are present in the Temple and immediately acts to cast them out. We, too, should be examining our lives and asking the question: "What are the distractions and idols in our lives that draw our attention away from our Heavenly Father?" Notice that I don't ask if there are distractions and idols. All of us, by virtue of our fallen nature, are fickle and easily distracted by the cares and concerns of the world. Let us, this Holy Week, rededicate ourselves to the difficult task of examining ourselves and casting out, with God's help, the obstacles to our relationship with God.

Lastly, Jesus reminds his disciples and the religious authorities that His Father's house is to be a house of prayer. Let us not be distracted by the beautiful liturgies offered this week, as if the liturgy were an end in and of itself. Let us not turn the liturgies into performances designed to entertain and dazzle the audience, but rather let us enter into the liturgies as a means of delighting our Heavenly Father. Sadly, even our form of worship can become an obstacle to the very thing we desire – a saving relationship with Jesus Christ. This Holy Week, let us approach the beautiful and intricate liturgies of the season as a means of transporting us to the foot of the cross, to the feet of Christ, and to the throne of Grace.

THE RT. REV. DR. ERIC VAWTER MENEES,
VTH BISHOP OF THE DIOCESE OF SAN JOAQUIN
The Rt. Rev. Dr. Eric Vawter Menees was consecrated to be the Vth Bishop of the Diocese of San Joaquin on September 24, 2011. Prior to his election, Fr. Menees served as the Rector of the Anglican Church of the Resurrection in San Marcos, California. Bishop Menees is married to Florence Guadalupe Mira-Menees and has a daughter, Milagro, aged 21 and a son, Sebastian, aged 14.

Meditation Forty-One

First Psalm: Psalm 51:1-18; Psalm 51:19
Second Psalm: Psalm 69:1-23
Old Testament: Jeremiah 12:1-16
New Testament: Philippians 3:1-14
Gospel: John 12:9-19

Our liturgical tradition offers us the daily opportunity to formally ask the Lord to forgive us for errant things we've done and things we've left undone. Because we find ourselves consistently repenting for the general sin of not loving Him with our whole heart and failing to love our neighbor as ourselves, we also face the possibility of forgetting the specific ways we've injured the Lord and His people. Thus, we risk not learning from our mistakes and potentially repeating them.

St. Paul lists several ways we distance ourselves from deepening our relationship with Christ while writing to the Church in Galatia, warning that embracing a sustained pattern of living in "…hatred, discord, jealousy, fits of rage, selfish ambition, dissensions, [and] factions" keeps us from inheriting the Kingdom of God.

Today's lectionary reading from John 12:9-19 displays the fruit of lives consumed by hatred, discord, jealousy, fits of rage, selfish ambition, dissensions, and factions, in part, to show us where those sins have taken root in our own lives and point us toward the One who can heal us.

Within the first two verses of the pericope, the bitterness of the Pharisees' hate claims its first victim: reason. Jesus called a dead man out of his tomb, gave him new life, and transformed one family's mourning into song; then, not only do the Pharisees want to murder Jesus for it, they decide they should kill Lazarus too.

The paradigm set by the first two verses becomes the overarching message of the entire passage. Sin blinds the mind and corrodes the heart, which in turn, leads to jealousy and fits of rage driven by selfish ambition.

If the appointed shepherds of God's chosen people not only rejected truth, but actively waged war against it while their Messiah physically walked amongst them, how much more prone to deception are we who live in an age where Jesus is not bodily in our midst?

This Lent, let us ask the Holy Spirit to purge us of any shred of hate so that no word or deed fueled by rage, jealousy, or selfish ambition could proceed from our lips or the work of our hands.

MR. JOSEPH PETER CALANDRA, JR., '17
Joe is married to Jaclyn and they have a son, Daniel Caleb, born October, 2014. Joe has served in the United States Air Force and holds a B.A. in religious studies as well as a M.A. in American Government, both from Regent University in Virginia Beach, Virginia.

Meditation Forty-Two

First Psalm: Psalm 6; Psalm 12
Second Psalm: Psalm 94
Old Testament: Jeremiah 15:10-21
New Testament: Philippians 3:15-21
Gospel: John 12:20-26

"Sir, we wish to see Jesus." These are the words spoken by the God-fearing Gentiles who had come up to the feast of the Passover and had heard of Jesus; this also should be the request we all hear as little Christs whenever we encounter others, for this is the sum and total of our work as Christians: to point others to Christ, who then points them to the Father.

But we often feel barren, empty, overworked and worn out by life and work, and when we realize that we have fallen short yet again, we cry out with the Psalmist, "O LORD, rebuke me not in your anger, nor discipline me in your wrath." Or perhaps we have been beaten down by others and this is our heart's cry: "Save, O LORD, for the godly one is gone."

No matter the depths of the wilderness you are wandering through this Lent, or even if you feel that you are soaring with the eagles, our Lord's answer is the same: "Truly, truly, I say to you, unless a grain of wheat falls into the earth and dies, it remains alone; but if it dies, it bears much fruit. Whoever loves his life loses it, and whoever hates his life in this world will keep it for eternal life."

You see, when we put to death our own appetites, our own desires for worldly glory and our own focus on earthly things, then that we can find life in Christ, and not just be brought to life, but we can become those who bear fruit for the Kingdom of God being transformed like Jesus from glory unto glory!

Would we see and show others Jesus? Then, like him, let us empty ourselves, seeking to first love God with all our heart, soul, mind and strength – for how can we give what we do not already have? Seek first his Kingdom and Righteousness! How do we do this? Here is a portion of St. Paul's direction to the church in Rome: "Let love be genuine. Abhor what is evil; hold fast to what is good. Love one another with brotherly affection. Outdo one another in showing honor. Do not be slothful in zeal, be fervent in spirit, serve the Lord. Rejoice in hope, be patient in tribulation, be constant in prayer. Contribute to the needs of the saints and seek to show hospitality" (Rom. 12:9-13).

Then, after we have found and loved our Lord and had our lives made over after the pattern of his cruciform life, we can be conduits of his love flowing back into the world. When asked to see Jesus, may our lives and words show the way!

THE REV. FORREST TUCKER, '13

Fr. Tucker serves as a church-planting rector at Church of the Incarnation in Billings, Montana, where he lives with his wife, Rebekah and their six children.

LENTEN
MEDITATIONS

MEDITATION FORTY-THREE

FIRST PSALM: PSALM 55
SECOND PSALM: PSALM 74
OLD TESTAMENT: JEREMIAH 17:5-10; JEREMIAH 17:14-17
NEW TESTAMENT: PHILIPPIANS 4:1-13
GOSPEL: JOHN 12:27-36

"Blessed are those who trust in the Lord, whose trust is the Lord. They shall be like a tree planted by water, sending out its roots by the stream. It shall not fear when heat comes and its leaves shall stay green; in the year of drought it is not anxious, and it does not cease to bear fruit" (Jer. 17:7-8).

The vast rocky wilderness and unrelenting sun and heat of the desert are physical elements that somehow expose the spiritual truths of our lives. Jeremiah understood this, but he also knew the hidden, abundant, and beautiful life of the desert—the plants and animals that thrive by the springs and small oases. So the desert became a ground of metaphor for him to describe the spiritual life.

In his Judean desert there grows a plant, known by the Bedouin as the 'cursed lemon.' In the rainy season it is a perfectly healthy looking shrub, which puts forth lovely fruit that looks like lemons. However its roots are shallow and it is so starved for water that when you break open one of the lemons you find only dry brown seeds. It is a dried up dying plant.

But by the springs and oases that dot the Judean desert grow fig trees. They sink their roots into the ever-flowing water; so that even in drought they find water and provide figs for the hungry and shade for the weary.

Jeremiah used these two different plants to illustrate a spiritual truth. People who reject God and put down shallow roots in worldly things are like the 'cursed lemon' shrub, spiritually desiccated, unable to grow into the fullness of who they were created to be, and having nothing left for anyone else.

Those who trust and sink the roots of their lives deep into God grow strong and whole, healthy enough to survive all the vicissitudes of life, even the driest times of spiritual drought, bringing forth fruit and able to give shade to the weary.

Jeremiah was, of course, speaking into the sin and situation of his day, but God's word is living and active, so his words speak to us still. As we take our spiritual journey through the desert this Lent, Jeremiah's words call us to examine our hearts, asking the questions, "Do we trust in the Lord? Are our roots sunk in the living waters of God?" In the deserts and droughts of this life, our answers to these questions make all the difference—will we grow strong in the living waters of the Lord or wither in the drought?

THE VERY REV. HEIDI KINNER, '04

The Very Rev. Heidi Kinner is a 2004 graduate of Nashotah House and currently serves as the Dean of St. Peter's Cathedral in the Diocese of Montana.

MEDITATION FORTY-FOUR

FIRST PSALM: PSALM 102
SECOND PSALM: PSALM 142; PSALM 143
OLD TESTAMENT: JEREMIAH 20:7-11
NEW TESTAMENT: 1 CORINTHIANS 10:14-17; 1
CORINTHIANS 11:27-32
GOSPEL: JOHN 17:1-11; JOHN 17:12-26

It's time. We've awaited this entire Lent not to finish with a countdown but to start counting up. Lent's 40 days culminate in the Great Three Days, the Triduum, which follow Jesus' Passover from death to life on the third day. In Hebrew reckoning, the three days to Easter Sunday begin on the Eve of Good Friday. That's tonight. Maundy Thursday evening begins the first day of the Triduum, the finale of Lent, the high point of Holy Week, and the hinge of the Christian Year. It's a lot to take in.

There's so much to take in, in fact, that groups of early Christians spent all night observing Maundy Thursday. It marked a night Jesus didn't sleep, so neither did they. Today's celebrations of Maundy Thursday follow the same ancient traditions of representing Jesus' momentous final acts before his death, especially the Last Supper and the foot-washing. Jesus prepared his disciples for the significance of his sacrifice unto death, with words and actions likewise significant. He gave them the context to understand, then later to celebrate, his passing through death as the decisive moment for God's glorious reign on earth as in heaven. This cosmic victory, this turning point of history, this glory is the focus of today's gospel for the daily office: John 17.

John 17 shows Jesus in prayer, the climax of his last discourse with his disciples before his agony. It's his longest recorded prayer, also known as his "high-priestly prayer" due to the parallels with the Levitical high priest's atonement offering. For us, beholding this scene is like getting VIP access to the intimate moment the disciples had with their Messiah. The vision of Jesus praying is an up-close and personal glimpse into the divine communion among the Godhead. The Son of God bared his heart, and we're within earshot. If we have ears to hear, we encounter his astonishing, life-changing proposal.

Jesus petitioned the Father, not just for the faithful eleven around him that moment, but for everyone who would come to believe through their word. That's us! We are included, not just implicated but directly mentioned, in Jesus' cherished desires for his friends. His words deserve our lingering attention today, for in them He gave the summation of his entire life and teaching. He prayed for our protection, joy, holiness, vision, unity, and most especially that the bond, the glory, the love of the Father and Son might be in us and we in them. This mutual indwelling is what we are in for. It's more than we can take in, because God longs to take us in. The revelation of John 17 is the invitation of the Triduum: Be taken in, today.

JENNIFER SNELL

Jennifer Snell is the author of the chapter on Holy Week for the resource guide Let Us Keep the Feast: Living the Church Year at Home (Doulos Resources, 2014). She worked in administration at Nashotah House, where her husband The Rev. Micah Snell graduated in 2008. With their three young children, they now live in Houston, Texas, where they serve at Houston Baptist University.

Meditation Forty-Five

First Psalm: Psalm 95; Psalm 22
Second Psalm: Psalm 40:1-14; Psalm 40:15-17;
Psalm 40:17
New Testament: 1 Peter 1:10-20
Gospel: John 13:36-38; John 19:38-42

Like the Samaritan woman, we all come to the well over and over again to draw water but I am not sure we all see the man sitting quietly there. Nor am I sure that we hear what he is saying to us. We are so busy bombarding him with our prayers, requests and, indeed, our praises that we take very little opportunity to sit and listen to him. If we could but hear we might find ourselves being asked by Jesus to do something for him. Jesus does not patronise us or look down on the poor and broken ones, the casualties of life. He does not initially come as one with something to give us. He does not come as one pretending to tell us how to live our lives. He does not start by saying, "Here, I have what you need. Take this and become like me." Instead Jesus tells the Samaritan woman that she has something he needs. She hears that there is something she can do for him and, hearing this news, she is liberated from all that weighs her down. He enters into a relationship with her first. He gives her value. He gives her purpose. He gives her new life by simply letting her know there is something she can do for him.

So for those of us who are eager to share our faith, this story challenges us to approach others in this way. This story challenges us to be willing to reveal our brokenness to these others and to Jesus. Jesus tells us that he is thirsty and then asks us to consider our thirst. If we are prepared to acknowledge our real thirst then Jesus can give us the living water that wells up to eternal life. As we continue our pilgrimage toward Holy Week, we remember that as John's gospel nears its conclusion on the cross, Jesus is still thirsty. He is still thirsty today. Do we offer him vinegar mingled with gall? Jesus is sitting before us this very minute, by the well. He is tired, very, very tired. He asks us to give him a drink. What shall we do? Jesus is hanging before us this very minute, nailed to a cross. He is in agony, he is near death. Again he asks us to give him a drink. What will you do?

Lord Jesus, you went not up to joy but first you suffered pain. You entered not into glory before you were crucified. Grant that we may walk in the way of the cross and find it none other than the way of life and peace. Amen.

THE REV. CANON JEREMY M. HASELOCK
PRECENTOR AND VICE-DEAN
NORWICH CATHEDRAL

The Rev. Canon Jeremy Haselock is Vice Dean and Precentor of Norwich Cathedral, England, and Chairman of the Diocesan Liturgical Committee. He is a Fellow of the Society of Antiquaries, a member of the General Synod of the Church of England, and the Cathedral's Fabric Commission for England. He was for ten years a member of the Liturgical Commission. His academic background is in History and Medieval Studies where he specializes in Liturgy, Iconography, Stained Glass and Architecture. Nashotah House conferred an honorary degree of Doctor of Music to Canon Haselock in 2013.

Meditation Forty-Six

First Psalm: Psalm 95; Psalm 88
Second Psalm: Psalm 27
Old Testament: Job 19:21-27
New Testament: Hebrews 4; Romans 8:1-11

Psalm 95 is a psalm that extols the kingship of Yahweh and in the process provides underlying reasons for trust and joy in Yahweh in the wastelands of life. It portrays the nurturing God of unlivable places, in the process depicting the emptying of entropy from the lives of God's people.

There are three strophes in this psalm, and it is both in the progression within each and in their verbal and thematic links that the message comes to articulation. These sections are (1) verses 1-3, (2) verses 6-7a, and (3), verses 7b-11. The first strophe begins with four exhortations to rejoice in God, the latter two segueing into bringing this joy into worship (verses 1-2). In verses 3-5, the psalmist writes that the reasons for this joy are the greatness of God and his control of the wild, uninhabitable places – the unexplored depths, the mountaintops, the sea, and the dry land. The sea is often a realm of chaos in the Old Testament and other ancient Near Eastern Literature. Written about in verses 4-5 in conjunction with areas that cannot support life, the sea also appears to share in this idea of an unlivable area.

Why God's control of these areas is a cause for joy is shown in the second strophe, which right away connects to the first by beginning in verse 6 with two more exhortations to worship Yahweh. The reason for this encouragement is that Israel is 'the people of his pasture and the sheep of his hand' (verse 7). Notice the links between the pasture with which God sustains his people and the unfruitful areas mentioned in verses 4-5. 'His' is used four times in verses 4-5 to refer to the barren areas as belonging to God and twice in verse 7 to speak about God's possession of the people he nourishes. Further, twice 'his hands' designates the former area of God's domain and once, the latter (verses 4a, 5b, 7a). The psalmist is intimating a theocentric obliteration of life-threatening and life-giving dichotomies.

In the third strophe the interweaving of the themes of the God of the infertile areas of existence (verses 1-3) and the God who nurtures his people (verses 6-7a) are brought together in the reflection on the incident at Massah and Meribah. There God showed his sustenance in the desert. Like the first two strophes, this one also begins with an exhortation, this one to trust God in their desert experiences (verses 7b-8).

The effect of this type of interlacing the two themes is to suggest that there are no impoverished areas of existence for the people of the God of these places; in the hand(s) of Yahweh is nourishment in desolateness. Joyful worship of Yahweh because of this realization supports trust in these times: the exhortations in verses 1-2 and 6 leading to the one in verse 7b. Underlying desolateness is a divine fecundity accessible by the specific character of the joy-infused trust articulated in Psalm 95.

DENNIS SYLVA, PH.D.

Dennis Sylva, Ph.D., is Adjunct Professor of New Testament, Nashotah House and Director of Lifelong Faith Formation at St. Jerome Church in Oconomowoc, Wisconsin.

Meditation Forty-Seven

First Psalm: Psalm 148; Psalm 149; Psalm 150
Second Psalm: Psalm 113; Psalm 114; Psalm 118
Old Testament: Exodus 12:1-14; Isaiah 51:9-11
Gospel: John 1:1-18; Luke 24:13-35; John 20:19-23

We live in a culture that, through public relations, creates an image or façade in order to convince or make a point, regardless of the truth. The twenty-fourth chapter of Luke, which announces the resurrection of Jesus, is a failure by our world's standards. As the chapter begins, the women go to the tomb to anoint the body of Jesus and find the stone rolled away. They encounter two men in shining garments who ask them why they seek the living among the dead. They remind the women of Jesus' teaching. When the women return to the eleven disciples, Luke responds that their words seemed to them like idle talk, and they did not believe them.

Next we have the two disciples traveling on the road to Emmaus. They were debating, and as they debated, Jesus joined them and asked why they were having this kind of conversation and why they were so sad. Cleopas is surprised that this stranger knew nothing of the crucifixion of Jesus of Nazareth, a prophet whom they had hoped would redeem Israel. They tell him of the women going to the tomb and how they did not find him.

In return, Jesus patiently teaches them of the Christ and how he had to suffer these things to fulfill the promises of the Scripture. When they near Emmaus he goes no further, and the disciples ask him to remain with them. At the table, he takes bread, blesses it, breaks it, and their eyes are opened.

It is incredibly difficult for the disciples to believe that the man they saw crucified is indeed the resurrected Lord. The witness of the Emmaus narrative is simply that we can trust that the resurrection took place. We see how slowly the disciples came to believe. Eventually, they come to see that, if God had power over Jesus' life and death, then God is in Christ, reconciling the world to himself.

That has been the witness of the Church through the ages, testified to by the blood of the martyrs not just yesterday but profoundly today. That's the joy of Easter.

I am blessed to live in a community of witness, Nashotah House Theological Seminary, where numbers of men and women sacrifice much to our resurrected Lord. They testify to his resurrection and the witness continues today. Christ is risen.

Christ is risen, indeed.

THE RT. REV. EDWARD L. SALMON, JR.

NINETEENTH DEAN & PRESIDENT OF NASHOTAH HOUSE THEOLOGICAL SEMINARY

Before his retirement from Nashotah House in 2014, Dean Salmon spent many years in ministry serving a variety of local parishes including St. Andrews in Rogers, AR; St. Paul's in Fayetteville, AR; and The Church of St. Michael and St. George in St. Louis, MO. Following this ministry Dean Salmon was elected Bishop of the Diocese of South Carolina in 1989 and served the Diocese until February 2008. More recently, Bishop Salmon served as Rector to the Parishes of All Saints Episcopal Church in Chevy Chase, Maryland and Christ Episcopal Church in Accokeek, Maryland. Bishop Salmon continues to serve as the Chairman of the Board for The Anglican Digest and has previously served on the Sewanee Board of Trustees, University of the South's Board of Regents, and as member and president of the board for Kanuga Conferences in Hendersonville, North Carolina.

Made in the USA
Charleston, SC
04 February 2015